A TIME TO RECALL

BY HELEN V. TAYLOR

A

TIME TO RECALL

The Delights of a Maine Childhood

———— ◆ ————

DRAWINGS BY ERIK BLEGVAD

W · W · NORTON & COMPANY · INC · New York

To NEIL, who was hunting for turtles' eggs at the trout pond when I was picking blueberries on the mountain. How fortunate that we met years later and now have sons and grandchildren to enjoy the old farm in Waterboro Center.

Contents

A TIME TO RECALL

ONE

Going to the Country

Grandfather's big white barn was joined to the house, as barns usually are in Maine. At the back of the barn was Nellie's box stall, and pushed against the side wall, with their shafts in the air, were Grandfather's buggy and the one-seated black sleigh. The surrey stood in the middle of the floor and Grandfather was getting ready to harness Nellie. Every inch in the surrey was crammed with boxes containing our summer things, for we were going to Grandfather's farm in Waterboro Center to stay until school started in the fall. A little earlier I had sat on Mother's Buffalo extension valise, bouncing up and down while she pulled the straps tight. Grandfather had pushed it into the only spot left free under the back seat.

In the backyard my little sister Susan was calling to Pinkie, our cat, who was hiding under the barn as if she knew she was about to take an uncomfortable trip. I ran to help catch her, giving a quick, joyful skip in anticipation of our ride. I was ten years old, a chubby little girl with a round face and two long braids of brown hair. I was happy to be leaving the red brick house on the quiet street in Saco. I was going to the country where a lake, a gentle mountain, and a big sunny house were waiting for me.

Now Nellie was harnessed to the surrey and Mother and Susan had climbed into the back seat. Pinkie, with her paws in a flannel bag, was mewing in Mother's lap. Susan's head was bent down as she talked soothingly to pussy. I ran eagerly to the end of the drive and held the long gate open so Grandfather could drive through. As I stood there by the horse-chestnut tree, I could look down the street to the white church which stood in the square below. The gold weathervane on top of the tall steeple gleamed against the blue of the sky. I thought back to the time, three years before, when I was only seven years old and Mother, Susan, and I first came to live with Grandfather in Saco. In those first months I often stood in this spot and looked down at the church because it made me think of that other white church in Biddeford where my father had been the minister. The ornate iron fence in front of Grandfather's house, the trim brick paved walk, and the heavy dark front door had all seemed stiff and strange. But now I looked around the yard with a happier feeling. Beyond the main house of red brick was a wooden ell, and attached to that was the big barn, both painted white. The neat lawn ran back to the vegetable garden and to the apple trees. The driveway led under these trees and I knew that in a minute Nellie and the surrey would come up to the gate. There would be a place for me right in the front seat beside Grandfather.

Grandfather had seemed like a very stern old man when we first came to live with him. Mother told me he didn't talk much because he had lived alone so many years with just Emma, his housekeeper. He was not nearly as tall as my father had been, but he stood so erect and kept his shoulders back so straight that I thought he was tall. He usually wore a black suit that was somewhat rumpled and the knees were a little shiny, but his stiffly starched dickey was very white and his tie of wide black silk was knotted carefully. His gray beard was short and neatly trimmed all around without any point in front. His eyes were dark gray and snapped from one thing to another so fast that I soon knew nothing escaped his attention, even though he said little. He kept a fat silver watch in his right vest pocket, and a thick gold watch chain went over to the opposite pocket where it was attached to a small pearl-handled penknife. I had come to marvel at the skillful way he used his penknife, slitting open envelopes so neatly that they didn't look as if they had been opened at all, or peeling a whole apple round and round with one long very thin peeling like a curl. Every day, after breakfast, Grandfather walked down the narrow brick path that ran through the garden to the iron gate that opened on the sidewalk. He would stand there with his thumbs in his vest pockets and look up and down the street. Mother said he did this because he had grown up in the country and people in the country always look to see what kind of weather the day will bring before planning their work.

It had been fall when we came to live in Saco, and the horse-chestnut trees by the gate were full of round prickly burrs which held the beautifully shiny horse chestnuts. I went out every morning to gather the ones that the wind and frost had shaken down during the night. But I soon discovered that if I didn't get there early, other children in the neighborhood would be ahead of me. I put them in my pockets and sometimes I gathered up my skirt and filled it with this treasure. I loved the smooth slippery feeling of the horse chestnuts and their glistening reddish-brown color.

Then came a day when I went to look for horse chestnuts and could not find any. Two boys outside on the sidewalk had a few in their hands, and I decided I had come too late. Then I heard a chuckle and looked over to where Grandfather was standing. His pockets were bulging and he had several large horse chestnuts in his hand. Without saying a word he beckoned me to follow him, and we went down the winding path to the barn where he had a workbench. With great deliberation he opened his penknife and made a hole in the center of about twenty horse chestnuts. Next he threaded them on a piece of string and tied the ends of the string together. I watched him with delight as he lifted up the chain and put it around my neck. "Go in and show your mother your necklace," he said.

From then on, every day after school and on weekends, I

followed Grandfather eagerly, helping him as he gathered the winter apples, Greenings, Russets, and Baldwins. The vegetable garden was behind the barn, but in the fall nothing was left in it but yellow pumpkins and the poles on which shell beans had grown. In the warm sun, the dried tomato and squash vines had a pungent smell. These Grandfather pulled up and piled with the leaves he raked away from the lawn. I carried armfuls of these leaves to the flower garden and piled them carefully around the rosebushes as Grandfather directed. Under the plum tree Grandfather showed me where I could occasionally find a plum that had lain hidden in the grass for a long time, and had grown soft and sweet and delicious. Grandfather pulled up the bean poles with vines still on them and took them into the barn. I helped him pull the vines off, and he gave me a penny for every pole I stripped clean. I got twenty-two cents that first fall, the most money I had ever earned.

My two long braids often got in my way as I ran after Grandfather, or climbed up on the limbs of one of the wide-spreading apple trees. In the morning Mother would tie a stiff bow of ribbon on the end of each of my braids but, too often, I lost one of these bows and couldn't seem to find it, no matter how hard I looked. Just before bedtime, Grandfather would often hand me the lost ribbon without saying a word, but with an understanding twinkle in his eye.

Grandfather always went to bed shortly after supper, but first he smoked his pipe for a few minutes in front of the living-room fireplace while he looked over the *Farmer's Almanac* to see what the next day would be. He always wore high leather boots that went up under his trouser legs almost to his knees. He used a bootjack to get them off, and I learned that he kept it in the sitting-room closet. I liked to bring it to him, and sit on the rug beside his chair as he put his heel in the hole at the end and pulled hard. His face would get very red and as the boot came off he gave a long "Ah-h-h." I had been holding my breath, and I also said "Ah-h-h."

The remembrance of those days of getting to know Grandfather flitted through my mind as I waited at the gate, but suddenly Nellie was beside me and it was time to close the gate and get into the surrey. I climbed into the front seat beside Grandfather and we were on our way. Mother and Susan had a thin robe over their knees and I pulled one up over my lap. The city street of hard packed dirt was dry, and as Mr. Green, our grocer, drove rapidly by in his open delivery wagon, he stirred up a cloud of dust. A little further along, Mrs. Rogers passed us. She had the most elaborate carriage in our town. It was called a Victoria, an open carriage with a deep comfortable seat. The coachman sat on a high seat in front and drove the two fine-looking black horses. Mrs. Rogers was a friend of Mother's and waved as she went by.

We were going slowly, for Nellie was old and we knew it would take us nearly four hours to cover the fifteen miles of winding country road to Waterboro Center. Grandfather held the reins loosely in his lap. The whip, with a red ribbon tied around it, swayed gently in the whipstock, but Grandfather, we were sure, would never use it. I looked around at Mother and she smiled and patted my shoulder.

Our street led into the open country and then the road wound in a leisurely fashion by fields and farms and through pine woods. There were hills where the wheels slipped on the pockets of small rocks and an occasional flat, very sandy spot where Nellie's heels raised puffs of dust and the wheels sank in with a grinding noise.

The sun shone down on us and the warmth enfolded me in a pleasant haze. In the cool shady spots the smell of the pines was strong. We were going slowly enough to look in under the trees where the light was soft and green and where ferns grew around half-buried rocks. Sometimes I caught a glimpse of a little brook running over moss-covered stones and I wished I could climb out and explore. At intervals along the way were irregular stone walls. Often they were tumbled down and poison ivy and wild rosebushes grew over them pushing the stones apart. Occasionally a meadow lark flew up beside the road. Mother said its brief sweet song was a greeting to us. Mother, Susan, and I played Wayside Cribbage part of the way, counting all the farm animals we could see and hopefully looking for a cat in a farm window that would count one hundred points. Grandfather did not join in our game but once or twice he nudged me gently with his elbow and nodded his head almost imperceptibly when he saw, at the far edge of a field, a cow or horse which had gone unnoticed in the back seat.

We met almost no one. If a farmer in his heavy wagon passed us, Grandfather would raise his hand and say, "How be ye?" And if someone hoeing corn in a field lifted his head to watch us pass, Mother and Grandfather would nod gravely. There were two long hills where Grandfather asked Susan and me to climb out and walk so that Nellie's load would not be so heavy. Susan picked some of the sweet fern and passed it up to Mother to smell. I knew Mother liked to chew the tender reddish leaves of checkerberry and I picked a bunch of these for her. To our surprise Nellie seemed to walk faster than we did and we had to hurry to keep up with her.

This was my third summer trip to Waterboro and by now there were landmarks that I looked forward to seeing. Among them were two brooks which crossed the road. Grandfather always pulled Nellie up on the long plank bridge of the first brook. We knew exactly what to look for. The bridge was shaded with thick willow trees, and a little below the bridge, on Grandfather's side, was a wide-spreading hemlock tree that leaned over a deep pool. The water was almost black. We would sit there quietly, not speaking, for perhaps five minutes. Then a trout would jump for a bug that had fallen from the tree. Without saying a word, Grandfather would slap the reins and Nellie would start on.

At the second brook the water was very shallow and a hard-packed dirt road led down beside the bridge into the water. Nellie seemed to know this was her chance to get a drink and always turned off the main road and walked into the stream. It came up on the carriage wheels about five inches, and Nellie stood there with little ripples around her legs drinking the cool water that ran quite swiftly over smooth granite pebbles.

At the Four Corners, about six miles before we reached

Grandfather's farm, we passed a small yellow house attached to a store. A big woman was standing on the porch energetically shaking a rug.

"There's Emma!" I said. Neither Grandfather nor Mother replied. Grandfather gravely raised his hand, but Emma flounced her big full skirts and walked into the house without seeming to see us. Emma had been Grandfather's housekeeper for nine years before Mother, Susan, and I came to live with him. She had expected to stay with Grandfather all his life and to be the manager of his house.

Emma had often seemed cross to me because she always said sharply, "Wipe your feet," when I came in from out of doors. She made me homesick for the gray shingled parsonage we had left. There the window shades were rolled way up so that the sun shone on the light oak furniture and on Mother's gay red-and-blue Sorrento scarf which was draped on the sitting-room mantel. I could run through the rooms if I wanted to and shout if I wanted to and Mother had smiled a lot and we all were happy.

It was the parlor shades that caused the trouble as far as I could see. Mother would go into the parlor and pull them up, letting more light into the dark room. But in a few minutes, Emma would come in and pull them down. After a bit, Mother would again raise the shades and when Emma saw it she would pull them down.

Mother took out Grandmother's Lowestoft china which was in a box in the dining-room closet and arranged some of it on the sideboard. Emma remarked in Grandfather's hearing, "Dangerous place for nice china with children around."

The next morning Grandfather walked into the parlor and looked around as if he were seeing it for the first time. The big square piano was closed and a green plush cover with a gold fringe was spread over it. He pushed the cover back and opened the piano just as Emma came in. "I think this must stay open," Grandfather said. "The children will be taking music lessons soon and these shades have to stay up so they can see." And he put the shades way up and stalked out of the room.

Two weeks later Emma went for a visit to her cousins in Alfred and never came back. Just a few months later she married the storekeeper at the Four Corners. Much of Grandfather's sternness seemed to melt away after that and Mother seemed less worried.

It was not long after leaving the Four Corners that we began craning our necks to see our mountain. It was really only a generous hill but, to us, it stood for the Alps and the Rockies. It rose from the pine woods with dignified slopes to a summit covered with granite boulders, and because no other mountain was nearby there was an exceptional view waiting for us when we climbed to the top. We could see the White Mountains of New Hampshire to the west and a thin streak of ocean to the east. The mountain was our friend, the guardian of our summer home, and after our winter in school and our long ride we shouted for joy. "I see the mountain, I see the mountain!" Our excitement seemed to puzzle Grandfather, but we knew that Mother shared our feelings. Pretty soon we came to Grandfather's woods. Tall white pines had grown there in Great-grandfather's day, but they had been cut down years ago for masts on the schooners that were built in Kennebunkport. The woods, as we knew them, were pitch pine with a few oaks and a border of white birch trees. On the banks under the birches, low bush blueberries and huckleberries grew. We always leaned out to see if the crop was going to be good. At the end of the woods was the hollow where the sweet wild strawberries were to be found and, just beyond, the field where the gypsies sometimes pitched their tents. I hoped with a little shiver, half of fear and half of pleasure, they would come back this year.

The field led up to the house and now we could see the generous barn and the big square house facing the mountain. In front of the house was a line of sugar maples and down over the hill in front was the silver line of the lake. At this point we could hardly sit still in our seats. Nellie, too, was anxious to end the long ride so, to our relief, she trotted the last quarter mile.

We drew up beside the house and the minute Grandfather said a long "Whoa-oa-oa" we children jumped to the ground and waited impatiently while he pulled from his pocket the heavy brass key to the green front door. We had to get acquainted with every room of the house which had been closed for the long winter. First, a dash into the sunny sitting room. The grandfather clock in the corner, the open cupboard over the fireplace filled with pewter and luster china, the round table with its big kerosene lamp, the comfortable Boston rockers, all were unchanged since we had left them.

The dining room beyond seemed to welcome us. The wide boards of the floor were painted pumpkin yellow and in front of the deep fireplace was the blue drawn-in rug with its cheerful wreath of red roses. Grandfather always insisted that the rug stay in place during the winter and the furniture remain in its customary position. In the fireplace was a crane from which hung two heavy iron pots, and at one side was the door of the brick oven which, years before, had been used for baking. Several fat ears of Grandfather's best yellow corn, their husks carefully braided, hung from a hook by the oven. The long wooden handle of a brass bedwarmer leaned against the bricks. In the window stood Great-grandmother Abigail's spinning wheel.

Had any swallows fallen down the chimney, we wondered? We rushed to see. The parlor was looked into hastily. We did not love this room. Its stiff furniture was covered with horsehair. In the window was a marble-topped table on which stood a Rogers Group called "Going to the Parson." Beside it were daguerreotypes and a fat photograph album with a dark red plush cover. A glass globe covered a basket of wax fruit. The grapes looked good enough to eat. But we must run to see if the kitchen pump worked. Could we get a cold drink after our long ride? We had only started exploring when Grandfather said sternly, "Come, Come!" and we knew we must help unload the carriage.

TWO

Great Aunts and Uncles

Great-grandfather's picture hung in the parlor of the farm. He was a bigger man than Grandfather but I thought the two looked very much alike. He had come to Waterboro Center from Alfred Gore when he was a young man and had built a store in the village at the place where six roads come together.

Before long he owned many timber lots and a good part of the lake shore. People came to his store from all the towns around. Mother called him a good Yankee trader and she said that at Thanksgiving time he used to buy pounds and pounds of butter and quantities of eggs from the farmers. Then he loaded up his big wagon and drove to Kennebunkport where he put it all on a coastwise schooner and went with it to Faneuil Hall Market in Boston.

After a while Great-grandfather hit on another scheme for making money by bringing sale work from Boston to Waterboro Center. From a manufacturer in Boston he got dozens of men's coats, pants and vests which were cut out but not finished. Farmers' wives were glad to earn money by sewing these garments at home. Great-grandfather drove around for many miles to find women who wanted to do this work. It was such a success that the store had to be enlarged and four or five men worked much of the time just inspecting and pressing the clothing before it was sent back to Boston.

It seemed strange that this could have happened in our quiet little village, but when I asked Grandfather about it, he reminded me that this was before the Civil War when Waterboro Center was a much more important town.

The Waterboro farmhouse had six bedrooms upstairs and two downstairs. Grandfather once told me the reason there were so many rooms was because it was built by his father to take care of all his children. Even when it became Grandfather's house, his brothers and sisters still thought of it as their home, and some of them returned each summer to visit us. They were my great aunts and uncles and, at times, they seemed like very old people to me, especially when they were fussy about food and drafts.

We called the bedrooms in the house by the names of the great aunts and uncles who had slept in them when the house was built in 1850. Aunt Lu and Aunt Addie visited us regularly and always took over the rooms they had had as girls. Uncle Alonzo also slept in his boyhood room. I knew the small bedroom at the top of the back stairs had once been Uncle Albert's and the two bedrooms downstairs had belonged to Grandfather and Uncle James. There was no room named for Anzolette, Uncle Lon's twin sister, because she had shared Aunt Lu's room before marrying and moving out West. Mother, Susan and I made a very small family so it was fun to imagine the house filled with Grandfather's brothers and sisters.

At the top of the front stairs were two connecting bedrooms which Susan and I occupied when there was no company. The front one was "Aunt Lu's room," and the back one where I slept was "Aunt Addie's room." I thought her bed was the prettiest one in the house. The bedstead was painted black with a pattern of gold oak leaves on the headboard and footboard, and the same design was on the bureau. Aunt Addie had knit the bedspread years ago and it was a little worn. When she was not visiting us, it was kept in the bottom drawer of the bureau. There was a small blue china jar filled with faded rose leaves on the bureau and I loved to lift off the cover and smell their musty, pungent fragrance. This treasure was always left in its place even when Aunt Addie was not visiting us.

Aunt Addie was a quick, little woman with snapping brown eyes and brown hair that she piled on top of her head with a row of short curls, in bangs, across her forehead. She always wore an ornamental tortoiseshell comb, which stood up stiffly in her hair to give her height. There were only a few streaks of gray in her hair and she was very proud of this fact.

Though Aunt Addie's hair had a soft wave, she wanted her bangs to be curled up tight. I liked to watch her curl them. Mother kept a row of small glass kerosene lamps on a shelf in the kitchen and at bedtime each grownup lighted a lamp and carried it up the dark stairs. In the morning the lamps were brought back to the kitchen to be filled with oil and, if the chimneys had become smoky, to have them washed and the wicks cut evenly across. We children were never allowed to carry a lighted lamp, but as I watched Aunt Addie walk through the hall with her lamp at a dangerous slant, I thought I could be at least as careful.

To curl her bangs, Aunt Addie stuck her curling tongs in the top of her lamp and the bulge of the chimney held them in place just above the flame. When she thought the tongs were hot enough she tested them on a piece of newspaper and if that turned brown, or smoked as if it was about to catch on fire, she waved the tongs in the air to cool them. Occasionally, she didn't wait long enough and singed her hair. For a day afterward she carried around a faint smell of burnt hair and some short, scorched ends would show in her bangs.

Aunt Addie wore black dresses and around her neck she usually tied a black velvet ribbon with a small cameo pin fastened on the front. Attached to her belt was a small black chatelaine bag in which she kept her eyeglasses and handkerchief and a small, flat green glass bottle of smelling salts.

On the parlor mantel there was a daguerreotype of Aunt Addie made when she was sixteen years old. I could see that she had been a very pretty girl. The picture showed her leaning on a table with her hands folded in front of her. Her hair was parted in the middle and a long, smooth curl hung down on either side of her face. She had a high forehead and beautiful eyes.

As an old lady Aunt Addie was like a little sparrow. She chattered and chattered and much of what she said was about herself. She was curious about everything and when a team went by the house she quickly went to the window and stood at one side, partly concealed by the curtain, and told us little details about the passerby. If Mr. Dennett drove down the road in his new wagon Aunt Addie was sure he had sold another woodlot, or if a woman had a pretty new hat Aunt Addie said that she had probably bought it with her egg money or, perhaps, her husband had got a good price for hay. If something surprised her, she would throw her hands up and say, "Land sakes!"

Mother was always ready with a nod or a "yes" but I don't think Grandfather heard a word. Aunt Addie's gentle voice flowed on and on, around us and beside us, and she didn't often expect a response.

Sometimes Aunt Addie joked with me and she pretended we had a secret together. When she was visiting us and I had moved into the little bedroom behind hers, we made believe that we were tapping messages back and forth to each other on the wall. Sometimes, too, on a rainy day, when I had to stay inside, Aunt Addie would get the big album of family pictures from the parlor and pull me down beside her on the sitting-room sofa while she told me about her brothers and sisters. If I didn't have to sit still too long, I liked to listen to her stories about going to quilting bees and about the big country store her father owned and how a thousand men had drilled in the field behind the house at the time of the Civil War. (It was hard to believe that so many men lived near the Center then.)

Great-uncle Alonzo and Uncle James had both fought in the war and Uncle James had been an officer in the Union Army. There was a picture of Uncle Albert in the album which had been taken in California. Aunt Addie showed me a ring he had sent her with a rough gold nugget mounted in it. Aunt Lu, I knew, had a similar ring. He was a heavy man who looked a little like Grandfather, only his beard was not neatly trimmed but was thick and bushy. Just in front of his ears were round, fluffy tufts of hair that looked like pieces of cotton that had been glued on. I could only remember his coming to Waterboro once, and then he and Uncle Lon had gone off fishing most of the time. There was a picture of Grandfather holding me when I was a baby. Mother told me the picture was a joke on Grandfather because he had refused to have his picture taken but was willing to hold me while the photographer took me. He didn't realize that he would show. He was smiling down at me and all the stern lines of his face were gone.

Aunt Lu was the oldest sister in the family. She was much taller than Aunt Addie, a thin woman with plain features. She didn't try to make herself pretty as Aunt Addie did. She, too, wore a black dress but with a severe high collar and a very full skirt that came down to the floor. Over this was a plain white apron with a deep hem. Somewhere, in the folds of her skirt, was a pocket, and, occasionally, she would mysteriously bring out a hard white peppermint and put it in my hand. I sometimes hung around her hoping for this sweet treat. In the window of Aunt Lu's room, which looked toward the lake, was a comfortable Boston rocker and often, when Aunt Addie was chattering, Aunt Lu would withdraw to this chair and knit quietly on her afghan.

Susan liked to sew and, although she was younger than I, she could make a much better seam than I could. The big, white aprons Aunt Lu wore were hemmed with such fine stitches that I could hardly see them. Sometimes Susan would sit by Aunt Lu and try to make the same tiny stitches in the hem of a doll's dress. Susan did not like to be left behind when I ran upstairs, and once she was so close behind me that she grabbed the bottom of my skirt and pulled out all the pleats from the waistband. This upset us both but Aunt Lu said, "Never mind," and mended the dress perfectly before Mother saw it.

Behind the washstands in the aunts' rooms were embroidered towels pinned to the walls to prevent splashing the paper. Each morning after breakfast, Susan and I were supposed to collect the water pitchers from the bedrooms and take them to the kitchen to refill them from the pump. First, I would pump twenty strokes and then Susan took a turn. The job took quite a time, for we not only filled the bedroom pitchers, but there was a tank on the back of the kitchen stove that had to be filled. We were warned to be especially careful of Aunt Lu's blue spatterware pitcher and bowl.

Aunt Lu lived with Aunt Addie in Portland and they both were widows. I had seen pictures of Aunt Addie's husband, but none of Aunt Lu's and it was hard to believe that she had ever been married. I felt a little guilty because I thought she looked like the picture of the old maid in our game of cards. But this was before Mr. Bradford told me about her.

Mr. Nathaniel Bradford was an old friend and former neighbor of Grandfather's who had become a wealthy businessman in Boston. He spent part of the summer nearby at Pleasant Pond. Once a summer he drove over to see Grandfather and everyone in our village wanted to get a glimpse of him. He came in an open carriage driven by a coachman and his two black horses with their braided tails and shiny coats were an unusual sight.

Mr. Bradford was short and fat and his round red face was sunk between his shoulders. He looked as if he didn't have a neck. His thick gold watch chain stuck out on his fat stomach. He had a hearty, booming laugh which made him shake all over. I think he liked to have Grandfather see how prosperous he was and he always spoke about the times he used to sweep out Great-grandfather's store when he and Grandfather were boys together.

The Bradford farm had been next to Grandfather's many years before and I thought Mr. Bradford must feel sad to see nothing left of it but an empty cellar overgrown with grass. I guessed that the empty cellars by the side of some of the narrow country roads near Waterboro had once belonged to the homes of friends of Mr. Bradford and Grandfather.

There was a little cricket by the window in the sitting room and I liked to sit there while the two old friends smoked their pipes after dinner. I listened curiously as Mr. Bradford recalled his job at Great-grandfather's store, how he had often harnessed the horses at two o'clock in the morning to drive the big farm wagon, piled high with firkins of butter, to the Portland market, and how he used to take trips to Kennebunkport with chickens and turkeys to send by boat to Boston at Thanksgiving and Christmas time. This was before the Civil War when Waterboro Center was really the center for all the country towns around and the store was a busy place.

I was eager to hear Grandfather speak of the sale work which his father had brought down from Boston every three months.

"Do you remember Mrs. Littlefield?" he asked Mr. Bradford once. "She lived behind the mountain. She could churn butter and do her chores and then sew five pairs of pants a day. We paid her twenty-five cents apiece."

"And I had to press them all!" Mr. Bradford chuckled. "There were four or five of us pressing men's suits for most a week before your father took them back to Boston."

Once or twice Mr. Bradford stayed with us all night. Mother gave him Uncle Lon's bedroom and his coachman went down to the Tompkinses who took in boarders. On these evenings Grandfather asked Captain Jones over after supper and the three men and Mother played sixty-three. I was allowed to watch them for a little while before I had to go to bed and Mother let me pull a chair up beside her.

In this game certain cards counted up to sixty-three and it was important to get a king because that was worth the most and counted twenty-five. Grandfather would look out of the corners of his eyes at Captain Jones and Mr. Bradford and would bid without picking up his hand. Captain Jones would get red in the face and very excited, but I could tell that Grandfather was really only teasing the other players. He almost always found a king when he finally picked up his hand and at times Captain Jones would get so mad he would fling his cards down and start for home, but Mr. Bradford usually persuaded him to come back.

Mr. Bradford always went to the cemetery on his day in Waterboro. It was a small enclosure behind the town hall. The neat stone wall around it had been partly paid for by Mr. Bradford. Once he asked me to walk up with him and when we got inside the cemetery he talked to me as if I were a grownup. He told me about his family and the old friends he knew when he lived in Waterboro Center. Finally he stood still by the corner of our lot and said, half to himself, "Lucinda is a brave woman."

"Aunt Lu?" I asked in astonishment.

"Yes, your Aunt Lu has had a sad life." He was looking at a row of small white marble gravestones that I had never noticed specially. A little white marble lamb was cut on the top of one. I knelt down and read, INFANT SON OF LUCINDA AND IVORY LIBBY, FOUR MONTHS OLD. The next one read, INFANT SON OF LUCINDA AND IVORY LIBBY, TWO MONTHS OLD. The third one was a little bigger and on the top was the figure of a child lying as if asleep and holding three lilies in her hand. It read, MARY, DAUGHTER OF LUCINDA AND IVORY LIBBY, THREE YEARS OLD.

"I remember when Mary died," Mr. Bradford said. "She had smallpox, but at first no one knew what the matter was and some children were brought in to catch measles."

"Why did they do that?" I asked.

"They used to think it was a good idea for children to have measles when they were young. When the doctor decided Mary had smallpox everyone was scared. There wasn't any vaccination then and the evening Mary died the folks thought she ought to be buried right away. I helped Ivory fix a little box. We couldn't paint it but we made it ship-shape and Lu lined it with some silk from one of her dresses. Then we dug this grave and your grandfather drove to Alfred to get the minister. We stood around the grave while he read from the Bible. I held a lantern for him to see. It wasn't long after that," Mr. Bradford continued, "that Ivory went to war. He got dysentery on Sherman's march to the sea and died in Georgia. Lucinda never talks about any of this. You would never know."

I looked at the three little graves with their small white stones, so lonely in the green plot, and suddenly I wanted to run back to the house and find Aunt Lu.

Uncle Lon was our favorite great-uncle. I thought he looked like the pictures of Uncle Sam. He was tall and thin and wore a mustache and a little goatee. He had merry eyes and loved to tell jokes. He also liked to show he was not old by dancing a little jig now and then, even though his legs wobbled and Mother was afraid he would fall. He lived twelve miles away in Sanford and came to see us frequently.

Uncle Lon's room was in the ell of the house and one of its doors led into the corn chamber and that, in turn, opened into the barn chamber. When Uncle Lon was not visiting us, a quick way to get out of doors without being seen was to dash through his room and the corn chamber and on out to the barn.

Mother never let anyone else use Uncle Lon's room, except for the few times Mr. Bradford slept there. The furniture in it belonged to Uncle Lon. Most of the Waterboro beds had heavy rope woven back and forth between the side pieces. A mattress filled with corn husks rested on the ropes, and on top of that was a feather bed. But Uncle Lon's bed, which was a pine fourposter, had a spring and a hair mattress. He had sent them to Waterboro from Portland.

Uncle Lon loved to fish. The boathouse at the lake belonged to him and so did the boat. He especially liked to fish for pickerel and to catch the big ones he needed someone to row the boat slowly while he trolled. Mother had taught me to row our very first summer at Waterboro. When Uncle Lon asked me to row for him I jumped up and down with delight. He usually said, "Want to go fishing with me?" and I quickly got my fishpole ready, knowing all the time that I probably would not fish at all—and not caring because it was such fun to watch Uncle Lon. He always chose the time for fishing with great care. He said that if the wind was ruffling the water too much the fish would not notice the bait and if the water was too still and calm, the fish could see us. Then, too, if it was hot and cloudless the fish went into the shadows under the banks of the lake or swam down into deep water where they could not be teased out.

The day we caught the big pickerel was a very exciting one. On that afternoon rain seemed near and the sky was gray so that the shadow of the boat blended into the green color of the water. There was a cove across the lake where the fishing was especially good. Several dead trees had fallen into the water and there were a number of tree stumps just below the surface. Lily pads and pickerel weed made a good hiding place for fish.

Uncle Lon picked out his bait carefully, sometimes it was a grasshopper which I had caught for him, sometimes a piece of salt pork rind. He skipped the bait along the surface of the water with quick short jerks that made it look exactly as if a small fish were jumping. He never seemed to get tired. If there was a sudden plop by some log, he would cast in that direction and when the line got slack he reeled it in with a chur-chur sound that was much like the scolding of the king-fisher way up in a dead maple.

Finally Uncle Lon stopped and said we should have some lunch. He had bought some crackers and cheese and ginger-snaps at the store and Mother had given me two bottles of homemade root beer. He stood his pole in the back of the boat and the end of the line, with its shiny spinner and piece of salt pork, sank slowly to the bottom. A fish never bites bait that is quietly lying on the brown leaves at the bottom, we thought.

My hands were red and hot from holding tightly to the oars. I had tried very hard to keep turning the boat in the direction which would help Uncle Lon. It seemed good to pull the oars inside the boat and to cool my hands in the water as we drifted very slowly toward a patch of water lilies. The big flat green lily pads covered the water in this part of the cove and among them were the beautiful, sweet-smelling lilies, their petals stiffly pointed and gleaming white, their centers butter yellow. I leaned over to pick some for Mother and this motion jerked Uncle Lon's line. The next moment the fishpole was almost pulled out of the boat. Uncle Lon grabbed it as the reel whirred, unwinding the line very fast. "Steady now," he said, "we've got a whopping big one."

I could see that he was excited and so was I. We couldn't see the fish but it was so strong that Uncle Lon had to let it run and then reel in a little bit at a time as it got tired. I rowed back when he told me to and we tried to keep the line from getting slack.

At one point, when the pickerel was far off beneath the lily pads, it tried to get under a fallen log and we were afraid a sharp stick or rock would cut the line. With great care Uncle Lon slowly worked it out into the open water and, as the fish got tired and turned over near the surface, we saw it for the first time. It was a beauty, long and slender and dark green with a sharply pointed head that helped it slice rapidly through the water. I didn't think Uncle Lon, or anybody, had ever caught a fish as big as this one. When he finally drew it near to the boat and passed the pole to me for a moment while he quickly put the net beneath the fish, it was so heavy he had to lift it with both hands.

Our first thought was to get back to shore as fast as possible to weigh and measure our fish and I rowed as hard as I could.

At the store the people waiting for the afternoon mail crowded around the scales as Uncle Lon lifted up the pickerel. It weighed four pounds and three ounces. Marsh Cousens, our storekeeper, said it was a record for our lake. When we got to the house, Mother saw me running toward her and thought something was wrong, but I shouted, "We've caught the biggest fish in the lake."

We went into the kitchen and Mother quickly put a long piece of brown paper on the table. Then Uncle Lon pressed the fish down to its full length and outlined it with a pencil. His hand trembled just a little so Mother carefully measured the distance from the nose to the tail. The pickerel was twenty-six inches long.

Uncle Lon took the outline of the fish up to his bedroom and pinned it on the wall beside his bed. Outside his bedroom, in the corn chamber, he had tacked to a low beam five or six similar pictures of prize fish, but this was much the largest and he wanted to see it each morning when he woke up. I knew it was partly my fish and every time I went by Uncle Lon's room I peeked in.

THREE

Nellie and Edgar

Grandfather did not allow anyone but himself to drive Nellie, and he never went on a ride for pleasure, so Nellie spent the summer in her yard behind the barn, growing fat and lazy on the thick grass and on the generous dessert of oats that Grandfather gave her when he put her in her stall at night.

Susan and I thought of Nellie as a member of the family and we loved to pull up tufts of clover from the field and feed them to her as we sat on the top rail of the fence that surrounded her yard. In Saco, too, it was fun to give Nellie a treat. We did this on stormy days when we were playing in the big barn chamber above Nellie's stall. Nellie's hay was on one side and in a corner were the three big barrels in which the winter apples were stored. I helped Grandfather pick the round, hard Greenings in the fall. They tasted very sour then, but by the middle of the winter their firm white centers were juicy and delicious. Grandfather's big buffalo robe was always spread over the tops of the barrels to keep the apples from freezing on cold winter nights.

Susan and I loved to slide apples down the hay chute secretly to Nellie and then kneel and peer way over the edge of the chute to watch her crunch the apples with her big white teeth and nod her head up and down in "Thank you." We were afraid to have Grandfather know we were doing this, but I think he probably knew. He would look at us shrewdly and say, "The winter apples must last till spring." This slowed us up, but after we saw him putting an apple in his pocket and going down to Nellie's stall we realized he, too, wanted Nellie to have her share.

Grandfather had a buggy with a black leather top and a seat upholstered in blue. He did not take this to the country because there was not room in it for three people and all our things, but he used it in Saco until the snow came. When Susan and I sat beside him in the enclosed buggy, we found much of the view was hidden by Nellie's fat sides which shook rhythmically as she walked or slowly trotted forward. Occasionally, she would switch her long tail and it would come up over the dashboard and get tangled in the whip-stock. We eagerly untangled it and pushed it back.

In the winter, it was fun to go riding in Grandpa's one-seated sleigh. This was painted black, with a line of red that made decorative swirls on the side, and a big red rose was painted on the dashboard. The streets were never plowed down to the surface of the road, and we slid along smoothly with the big buffalo robe covering us up to our chins, and often with a soft spray of snow blowing in our faces. The bells on the shafts of the sleigh and around Nellie's neck made a wonderful tune. I think Nellie liked it.

Our street was the longest straight street in Saco. A little way below our house was the square and the church and the soldiers' monument. In the winter, men who had fast horses and light cutters would gather in a field a mile up the street and race each other, often three abreast, to the monument. We loved to watch the snow fly out from the horses' hoofs and to see the men leaning way forward, shouting. We wished Grandpa would race Nellie. We always believed she could go much faster if Grandpa would just touch her with his whip.

The most exciting thing that happened to Nellie occurred one Memorial Day. A few days before this particular holiday we saw Grandfather rubbing Nellie down and combing her mane and tail very carefully. He did this for three days in succession, and we asked him why. He said that the city marshal's black horse was lame, and so he was going to borrow Nellie to ride in the Memorial Day parade. We could hardly believe our ears. Though we always had believed in Nellie, this was expecting a good deal of her. Grandfather reminded us that Nellie used to be in the circus, but we could see that Grandfather, too, was a little worried.

On Memorial Day morning, Nellie was once more carefully groomed.

"Would you like to use your red hair ribbon to braid in her mane?" Mother asked.

That seemed like the crowning touch, and we thought dear Nellie looked very splendid when a man led her up the street to the marshal's house where she was to be saddled.

Our house was surrounded by an ornate iron fence with granite posts. That morning Susan and I climbed up on the posts on either side of the front gate, high above the sidewalk. From there we could watch for the parade. It was to pass by our house and end in the square below.

We waited impatiently, and then our hearts sank. We saw Nellie coming down the street with her usual slow, ambling pace. I kept saying under my breath, "Come on— Oh do come on, Nellie!"

Henry, the boy who lived across the street and who knew Nellie very well, shouted teasingly, "Hey, is that your horse?!"

I felt my face growing red as the neighbors, standing on the curb of the sidewalk, turned and smiled. Then the leader of the band behind Nellie raised his baton, and the drums beat out the rhythm of a lively march. Nellie pricked up her ears and in a minute her back was arched and she was lifting her feet high in perfect time to the music. On she came proudly leading the parade. Now she was in front of us, and forgetting the people I shouted, "Hooray, Nellie!"

But Nellie did not look at us. She was hearing the music that had stirred her in her youth when she paraded with the circus.

Our neighbors on the sidewalk turned now to smile in approval. The city marshal saluted Grandfather who was standing by the gate.

Grandfather nodded his head and gave his low chuckle. Then he reached up to pat my hand. "Didn't I tell you?" he said.

Mother could drive very well, we thought, and it seemed a pity she couldn't use safe dependable Nellie to take us on rides along the country roads near Waterboro Center. We thought this even more emphatically after our trip to the trout pond, when Mother hired a horse and wagon from Mr. Tompkins. At first, Mother, Aunt Addie, Susan and I were happy to be going on this seven-mile ride to see our friends the Crandalls and to look at the trout, but we had a surprise in store for us.

Mr. Tompkins had two horses for hire. One was Sadie, who liked to amble along, sometimes stopping for five minutes beside the road to enjoy some clover. No amount of pulling on the reins hurried her. The other was Edgar, a young, rather skittish horse, who had a lovely brown coat and was quiet and gentle when Mr. Tompkins stroked his nose. Mother chose Edgar.

Mr. Tompkins' wagon had two seats and on each was a shiny black leather cushion. The seats were slippery, and when the sun had been shining on the leather, they were very hot. The wagon was high and it wasn't always easy to climb in. A tall man like Mr. Tompkins could put his foot on the hub of the front wheel and swing himself over the wheel into the seat, but Mother had to hold up her long skirts and put her foot first on a small round step between the front and back wheels, and then quickly take another step into the wagon. It wasn't easy for us children either to get the pleated skirts of our Peter Thompson sailor suits out of the way of that dusty wheel.

Mother and Aunt Addie sat in front and Mr. Tompkins held the horse's head because Aunt Addie was sure he would start before she could get settled with her robe over her black silk dress, and her small hat at the proper angle. Susan and I were in the back seat. When it was not in use, the back seat could be taken out, but now it was fastened to the floor of the wagon. Even so, if the horse gave a sudden jerk, the seat would move up and down and feel as if it were coming loose.

The country road was narrow and at first it led through the woods. There were white birch trees and hemlocks beside the road and at one place we went between two huge boulders covered with green moss and small hanging rock ferns. In this shady stretch, the sun could not shine through the trees and there were deep, wet ruts in the road. Mother tried to drive at one side of the road and avoid them, but sometimes a wheel slipped into a rut and the wagon swayed back and forth. Out in the sunshine the dry sand and gravel of the road clung to the wheels and sometimes was kicked up by Edgar into our laps. Mother held the reins high and watched Edgar closely, but after a while she began to feel more comfortable and when we reached a place where the road was smooth and hard, she urged him to trot. As we went through a covered bridge over the Saco River, Edgar's hoofs made a noisy "klop, klop" and in places the floorboards rattled. The bridge was dark but, through the cracks between the boards on the sides, we caught glimpses of the river flowing smoothly by.

Beyond the bridge was a curve in the road and, to our dismay, as we turned the corner, we saw an automobile approaching. It was red, with lots of shiny brass on the front, and as it moved toward us it seemed to fill the road. Edgar, like most horses, did not like it. He tossed his head, shaking the reins, and when Mother pulled hard so that he wouldn't get the bit in his teeth and run, he began to back. She tried to stop this by touching him with the whip, but he continued to back, twisting the wheels together so that we were afraid we would tip over. I remembered that Mr. Newcomb, a few weeks before, had met an automobile while driving a load of hay. His horse bolted into a neighbor's dooryard and a wheel of the rick caught on an apple tree. Over it went, pulling the horse down with it. Mr. Newcomb fell on the kicking horse, but he managed to scramble out of the way, unhurt. Was something like this going to happen to us?

Edgar was still backing in spite of anything Mother could do, and suddenly our back wheels went into a narrow ditch. There was a bank of bushes behind us, so for a moment we were standing still. Mother tried talking soothingly to Edgar and Aunt Addie, in a faint voice, was saying over and over, "Whoa, now, whoa." Susan and I held tightly to the front seat because we thought our seat might jounce out.

At this point, fortunately, the driver of the machine stopped, climbed out and walked toward us. He was wearing a long linen duster and a linen cap with a visor. In a minute we recognized him as Mr. Dennett, one of our neighbors in Saco. He came toward us slowly, speaking quietly to the horse. By now Edgar was standing still but he was trembling all over. We held our breath while Mr. Dennett took hold of the bridle and patted Edgar's nose. "I am going to lead him past the automobile," Mr. Dennett said. "Perhaps you would like to get out and walk."

But we all answered, "No, thank you." We preferred to stay in the wagon with Mother.

As we went by the machine, Edgar pranced sideways but he didn't try to pull away from Mr. Dennett. We saw Mrs. Dennett and a friend sitting high up in the back seat. They looked very nice with their linen coats and their hats tied down by long crepe scarfs. Mrs. Dennett leaned out and called, "I'm so sorry." We could see she was almost as frightened as we were.

We got safely past and, when Edgar quieted down, Mother regained her courage and we drove on again—not, however, without an uneasy feeling.

We arrived at the trout pond without any further excitement. We planned to eat a picnic lunch there and visit with the Crandalls who owned the pond. Mr. Crandall had moved to this spot for his health and we noticed that the fragrant fir balsams and the sweet ferns gave a delicious smell to the clear air. Mr. Crandall had bought the land around a small spring-fed pond and then had dammed up a brook to make three artificial ponds of different sizes. In these he raised trout to sell in the Portland and Boston markets. The water in the big pond was deep and the trout in it were living down by the cool, dark bottom, but the smaller ponds were shallow and, as we walked along the paths by the edge, the trout could feel the slight movement of the bank under our feet. They darted out from their hiding places and we could see the lovely red spots on their green sides. There were long soft grasses on the shallow bottoms of the ponds which swayed with the current and seemed to wave like green ribbons behind the darting fish.

Mother and Aunt Addie went up on the porch of the cottage to talk with Mr. and Mrs. Crandall, and Bill Crandall, who was about my age, took Susan and me around the ponds. He was a lively, friendly boy, eager to show us everything of interest. He had a pail filled with tiny pieces of liver and, when he threw a handful into the water, it looked as if it were raining as dozens of trout made little ripples jumping for the food. Then Bill told us to stand very still and he knelt by the bank and put his hand, filled with liver into the water. The trout rushed to get the food and for some minutes after it was gone, they swam through his fingers and even tried to nibble his hand.

There were many birds around the trout ponds, more, I thought, than around our lake. Maybe it was because the water was still and they could see plainly the bugs hovering above the surface. A bluejay scolded us and, for just a moment, I thought I saw the bright color of a scarlet tanager. On the further edge of one of the shallow ponds I noticed a blue heron standing motionless. Suddenly it stuck its long bill into the water and came up with a trout. Bill threw a stone and it slowly flapped its big wings and flew away.

"The heron and the mink get a lot of our fish," he explained, "and look up there!" High above us a big bird was soaring in swooping circles. Bill said it was a fish hawk and that it was hard to scare the hawks away although his father tried to do so by shooting his gun into the air.

As we walked along, Bill showed us the sandy bank where turtles laid their eggs in the spring. He said the eggs were round and white, about an inch through, and when one was dug up it felt like rubber. Sometimes he had seen a little turtle hatch out and the minute it was born, it started crawling straight toward the water. Then Bill took us behind the cottage to a small fenced-in yard where he kept his burro. He was a friendly little fellow and ran over to Bill when he was called.

"Is he afraid of automobiles?" I asked.

"He doesn't go out on the road," Bill said, "but we have an automobile ourselves. It's an Autocar. I'll show you."

We followed Bill into the barn and stood with wonder looking at his father's machine. It had a big brass horn and lots of brass trimming, and was so shiny it looked as if it didn't go out on the road either.

"I get twenty-five cents a week for shining it," Bill informed us. He showed us the crank in front which his father had to turn to start it, and he told us proudly that his father had recently changed a tire on the road in less than two hours.

While we ate our picnic on the porch of the cottage, Mr. and Mrs. Crandall listened to Mother's story of Edgar's fright and they had some suggestions for our return ride. They thought it was dangerous to let the horse back and said he should be urged past an automobile as quickly as possible. Mr. Crandall was very kind and even suggested driving us back, but Mother was rested by now and said she was not afraid. There were very few automobiles in the country and we were not likely to meet one again. The ride back started off quietly, but we still had an uneasy feeling about Edgar. Mother said if she saw an automobile coming she would turn off the road into somebody's yard. I knew we didn't pass many houses along the way, but I didn't say anything.

Mother drove with special care and we were within a mile of home when it happened again. From behind us, this time, we heard the dreaded "chug, chug" and the loud blare of a horn. We turned and saw a cloud of dust as a big, black automobile came charging after us.

Edgar was not going to be caught this time. Home was near at hand. He started running with such speed that the wagon rocked dangerously from side to side. Mother pulled on the reins with all her strength but it had no effect on him. I leaned over the back seat and put my arms around her waist to help keep her from being dragged over the dashboard. Aunt Addie covered her face with her hands and Susan hung onto me. Our seat buckled and bounced. Down the village road past our house Edgar dashed. He whirled into his own yard and went straight into the barn. One wheel nearly caught in the door as we went in. With his chest heaving and great flecks of white sweat over his sides, Edgar finally stopped, and for a moment we all just sat there.

Then Mr. Tompkins hurried into the barn. He looked at

Edgar, who was still breathing hard, and then looked disapprovingly at Mother, whose pretty sailor hat was askew and whose black skirt was covered with dust.

"I see you don't know much about driving horses," he said, then added sarcastically, "I suppose you had a good time!"

"Yes, we did," said Mother in a brave voice. She stepped down without another word and walked quickly out of the barn door. Susan and I followed right after her, but Aunt Addie found her voice and stayed behind to tell Mr. Tompkins a thing or two about Edgar.

FOUR

The Lake

Mother always spoke quietly. She had a kind, understanding manner toward everyone, but there was a spark inside her that made her fun to be with—something unexpected might happen. One summer night when the moon was full she called me out into the garden to look at it. It was warm, and the air was sweet with the smell of hay and the sharpened odor of flowers that had soaked up the sun. The moon, rising above our woods, was enormous—a great, red-gold platter. The crickets and katydids were very emphatic. The dirt road beside our field looked white in contrast to the black trees. Suddenly Mother held up her long skirt with both hands and called, "I'll beat you to the woods!" And she was halfway there, running with short, swift steps before I could untangle my clumsy feet and run after her.

Mother encouraged us to look for unfamiliar flowers in the woods. We brought them home and she pressed them in the flower book beside their names. She taught us the birds, too. Sister and I liked to go with her to a hemlock tree on the far edge of Grandfather's field and sit very quietly on the ground under the low-hanging branches, and wait for the warblers to appear at Mother's whistle. It was a wobbly, uneven whistle, but somehow it brought the chickadees, nuthatches and even the myrtle warblers.

I think Mother would have enjoyed swimming with us if she could have gotten over her fear of the water. One summer she bought a pretty bathing suit. It was black with a full skirt trimmed with rows of white braid. The blouse had little puff sleeves and, of course, she wore long black stockings. (I was glad she let me go in with my legs bare, but she said I would have to wear stockings when I grew up to be a lady.) Dressed in her new suit, Mother walked slowly into the lake until the water was up to her knees. She stood still for a few minutes, and we didn't dare splash her. Then she turned back and sat on the bank under the big pine tree. She said she would rather watch us and we knew we couldn't persuade her to try the water again.

But though Mother could not swim, she wanted us to learn both swimming and rowing. The boat belonged to Uncle Lon and was a slender Rangley skiff that cut through the water like a canoe, but still was wide enough to be safe. It was painted green. Mother sat in the back of the boat while she told me just how to hold the oars. They were spoon oars, and when I got so I could turn the boat skillfully and could give a long stroke and then let the back of the oars spank the water ("feathering," it was called), I felt very proud.

It was a rule that I must never go straight across the lake, but should reach any point of interest by skirting the shore. I liked to stay near the shore anyway because there was so much that was new and interesting on the banks.

The lake was about three and a half miles long, and it was an adventure to row all the way around. I had never done it alone until one summer when Mother surprisingly gave her consent. She made me a picnic lunch of sandwiches and apples and a bottle of root beer, and then she gave me a shoebox and said it was for "treasures." When I pulled away from the shadow of the tall pine by the boathouse, I felt like a real explorer.

For a short distance the bank was high and sandy. I could just see the tops of the pines that were behind it, but soon I rounded the point that brought me into Black Cove. It was called Black Cove because it was so surrounded by tall trees that the sun only shone on the water at noon. In the center the water was dark green-black, and I could not see the bottom. This cove was the deepest part of the lake.

I stayed close to the shore, and I could see way under the hemlocks that crowded the edge of the bank and whose wide lower branches looked like soft, lacy skirts. Spikes of yellow foxglove were growing right by the water. I knew they were rare and unusual, so I picked a spray to start my treasure box.

Halfway around the curve of the cove, three big white birch trees bent way over, almost touching the lake. As I came near, I pulled in the oars and took hold of a branch of the biggest tree. There was not a ripple, and the boat floated on its own clear reflection. By looking down into the shadow of the boat, I could see where the bank fell away under water in a nearly vertical drop. The soft green-blue color at the surface changed to brown where some big rocks lay, and then the bottom disappeared. Suddenly, the boat seemed thin as an eggshell. The lake was as deep as Grandfather's barn was high, and I was floating on it. What was at the bottom?

I stayed still, listening to two bluejays scolding, and I sensed the surrounding silence which the birds were interrupting. Then I saw a green perch swim by, slowly moving his little red fins. He was followed by a small school of minnows close to the surface. I put my hand in the water, and with an instant flick of their tails they vanished.

When I rowed out of the protecting circle of Black Cove, I found the wind was blowing strongly. Little waves capped with white foam seemed to run at me and slap the boat. I saw our mountain above the opposite shore looking green and serene, and there were no clouds in the deep blue sky, so I knew this was not a storm. It was a rowing contest between the wind and me, and I started to pull hard to make headway up the lake. I braced my feet and took long, strong strokes. My hands smarted, and the leather bracelets on the oars squeaked in the oarlocks. I kept very near the shore, but

I didn't look at it now. The wind was on my back, and I felt happy and confident and strong enough to row anywhere!

Mr. Roberts' grove was just ahead and was the first place I planned to stop. I pulled the boat up on a little sandy beach and walked in under the tall white pines. Mr. Roberts was very proud of these trees, which he called a virgin growth, and he kept most of the underbrush cleared out and the lower branches cut away so that the trunks looked like the masts of tall ships. Indeed, Grandfather had told me that these trees were like the ones his father used to cut on the mountain and haul to the shipyard in Kennebunkport.

I stood among them and put my head way back till I could see the sky through the branches and hear far above me the soft singing of the wind. The trees seemed very stiff and unbending, but when I looked closely I discovered they were swaying quietly for more than half their length. I wondered what it would be like to stand on the deck of a big ship, with a mast as tall as one of these pines and with the wind blowing a great white sail. I sat down with my back to a tree to drink some of my root beer, and the smell of the pines was all around me. The brown pine needles made a thick, soft carpet, but in places there were patches of green moss and the shining leaves of pipsissewa.

I rested there for a few minutes and then started out again toward Loon Island. A family of loons had lived near the island for as long as I could remember, but I had never been able to get very close to any of them, though I had often tried. Many times in the night I had heard a loon calling as it flew over our house. How could a loon find the lake in the night, I often wondered, as I snuggled down in my comfortable bed and imagined what it would be like to fly in the dark night to find my home?

The call of the loon was half a laugh and half a cry, a descending, clear note which I learned to imitate, "Who-o-ho-o, who-o-ho-o." Sometimes, standing on the point near our boathouse, I would call and a loon from way up the lake would answer. Sometimes, too, if I was rowing and saw a loon's dark head with its handsome white collar showing above the water, I would try to row in that direction. Suddenly, the loon would duck under. Then I tried to guess its location and rowed as hard as I could to be near it when it surfaced—but I never guessed right. I would see the loon floating calmly a long way off. The loons never seemed to try to get away by rising out of the water and flying, but they managed to stay under the surface for several minutes. Grandfather told me a loon was so alert and quick that it could see the flash of a gun as it was fired, and could get under the water before the bullet reached it.

But on this row up the lake I had unusual luck. The wind had died down as I neared Loon Island, rowing as quietly as I could. The little island had three pine trees on it and a jumble of huckleberry and blueberry bushes. Between the island and the main shore was just enough space for the boat to squeeze through. I gave one long, vigorous stroke and lifted the oars. As I shot through the narrow passageway, I suddenly came upon a mother loon and two babies. Immediately, far out ahead of me, there was a great splashing as the father loon half rose out of the water, flapping his big wings and calling in an effort to toll me away. The mother loon called to her babies to duck under, and she herself went down beside my boat, but the fluffy goslings were too young to stay under. They were so close that I could see them just below the surface, whirling around for a second and bobbing up.

By some mistake, the mother got on one side of the boat not more than an oar's length away, and the babies were on the other side, quite helpless and bewildered. The mother did not leave them, but called and called to them in a very frightened way. She flapped her wings and I could see plainly her beautiful black markings. Her notes were broken and despairing. I could easily have leaned over and picked up the little loons. They were so young that they were little balls of fluff. But the mother's brave, sad cries made me feel very sorry and I took two quick strokes beyond them. When I looked back, they had disappeared.

Blueberries and huckleberries grew on many banks of the lake. We called the huckleberries "black-snaps" because they were a shiny black and because each berry concealed a little seed that often made a snapping noise as it was bitten. I knew there was one sunny bank where the blueberries were usually thick. The field behind the bank was free of trees and was covered with juniper bushes and granite rocks. In the shadow of the rocks grew the biggest blueberries anywhere except, perhaps, on our mountain. I had brought a tin cup with me and intended to pick some berries as I sat in the boat.

A narrow brook, at this point, connected our lake with a

little pond. A canoe could go from one to the other, but it was too shallow for a rowboat. I had always wanted to try to get through with our Rangeley skiff, and now that I was alone and the boat was light, I decided to try it. The bottom of the passageway was sandy, and at first I had no trouble. Whenever I felt the boat scrape the sand a little, I took an oar out of the oarlock and pushed back into the deeper current. Halfway through, some alderbushes hung way over, hitting my head. Just beyond, I could see the brook was wider and I rashly decided that a few hard strokes would get me through. But I found I had driven the boat up on a sandbar. I wasn't distressed at first. Surely, by standing up and pushing with an oar, I could get free. But the boat didn't budge. There was nothing to do but get out and shove. I took off my sneakers and stockings and stepped out on the sandbar. The water came above my ankles and rippled around my legs. I could see the bottom of the boat was several inches down in the sand; but it was not until I had pushed and tugged for several minutes that I realized I was stuck fast. All sorts of perils flashed through my mind. I would have to stay with the boat until someone found me. I would starve to death or maybe, when night came, a wildcat would attack me.

Perhaps I could cross the field to some distant road and then walk for miles and miles until I got home and had to tell Mother I had lost Uncle Lon's beautiful boat. I pushed some more. It was hot in this cramped place with alderbushes and blueberry bushes hemming me in on both sides. Mosquitoes and little black flies found me and I had to stop to slap them. The sun shone down on a pail in the back of the boat which had held bait a few days before, and the smell came up in my face as I pushed. I threw the pail frantically into the bushes. The bottom of my gingham dress fell in the water, and its wet folds clung to my legs, my arms ached and I was ready to cry.

"I'll help you," said someone behind me. I turned quickly and saw a barefoot girl about my own age. She was holding a pail half full of blueberries in her hand, and this she put carefully down on the bank. She was a ragged little girl. Her cotton dress was faded and dirty and her hair was tangled and uncombed. She was very brown and, though she looked a little shy, she stepped out quickly into the water beside me. We put our shoulders together against the boat and dug our feet into the sand. Slowly, very slowly, the boat began to move, and when the sand gave a great sucking sound and suddenly let go, we almost fell forward on our faces. We looked at each other and laughed aloud with relief. We had been so anxious that we had scarcely spoken a word.

"Do you live near here?" I asked.

"Yes," she said, "at least our house is only two miles away but we own the rights to these berries. We take them to the Sanford market."

I was going to ask her more, but we could hear someone behind the alderbushes on the bank. The girl looked frightened and, picking up her pail, she moved quickly out of sight. I climbed into the boat and started to back toward the lake, and as I did so a big, rough-looking man stepped out on a stump.

"Go on with your picking," he said crossly to the girl. I wasn't sure whether a stick broke under his foot or whether he slapped her. I only knew I wanted to get out of the brook and into the lake as fast as I could. The man watched me for a minute, and I thought he was going to try to take hold of my boat. Then he called, "I guess there are enough berries here if you want to pick some."

"No thank you," I answered in a small voice, feeling a little scared and alone. As soon as there was room, I turned the boat around and started rowing rapidly up the lake, keeping well out from the shore.

For a while I kept my eyes on the trail of the boat in the water, now silver with a green lining, now all silver as it rippled off toward the middle of the lake. I wondered if it would go on and on for miles. That idea made me a little more lonely. Just for a minute I felt that my lovely day was spoiled, but I soon came around a little point and could see the end of the lake half a mile away. Once more I was an explorer and my goal was in sight.

This part of the lake was quite different from the shore near our boathouse. There were no trees and the banks on both sides were low and marshy with tall reeds growing in the water. I felt happy again as I saw the cheerful red-winged blackbirds flying in and out of the marsh. The water was shallow, except where the current moved swiftly toward the outlet of the lake. The purple blossoms of pickerel weed made a violet fringe on the green-waving scarf of the reeds. At the far end I pulled the boat up beside the small wooden dam which controlled the flow of water out of the lake and into Brown's Brook which, half a mile below, ran into the Saco River.

There had once been a grist mill at this spot. Nothing was left of it now except the brick wall on one side of the sluiceway, and the rotting remains of a big wheel. The bricks were overgrown with green lichen and moss, and the water oozed out between them and dripped into the pool below. There had also been a store and three houses here. Their cellars were filled in with a tangled mass of coarse grass and pink fireweed. Why had people left this lovely place, I wondered?

Down the brook a little way was Aunt Minnie Chase's house. She was not really an aunt at all, but I always called her "Aunt." I knew one reason Mother had allowed me to take this all-day row was her understanding that I would call at Aunt Minnie's. The house looked like the pictures of the witch's house in the story of Hansel and Gretel in my fairy-tale book. But Aunt Minnie was not like a witch; she was a very kind friend. The roof of her house rose to a high peak in front and then swept down on both sides nearly to the ground. It was a white clapboard house with three maple trees in front and a thicket of firs behind. It stood just below the site of the old mill which Aunt Minnie's grandfather had run many years ago.

As I walked toward the house, I could see Aunt Minnie standing beside the pool below the dam. She was older than Mother, a thin stooped woman who usually walked with a cane because she had rheumatism in her knees. She was picking sprays of mint. I ran to her and gave her such a big hug that she almost lost her balance. "I'm so glad to see you!" I said, thinking of the cross man who was picking blueberries. She hugged me back and looked a little surprised as she asked me if I was alone.

I told her all about my trip and, when she insisted that I eat lunch with her, I went happily into her big, comfortable kitchen where a small table stood in the window that looked out on the pool. Aunt Minnie had been making raspberry jam that morning and the glasses filled with this deep red, delicious treat were cooling on the wide windowsill.

The size of the pool just below Aunt Minnie's window changed with the amount of water that came over the dam. The right to take the boards off the dam belonged to the mills in Saco, and this was done when the river got low. The lake water flowed out in a sizable stream until way back at our boathouse we found our sandy beach growing much wider. Aunt Minnie was glad when the dam was high and her pool was a quiet spot where waterlilies grew and where mint was thick on the shore.

I sat down with her to eat lamb stew and thick slices of homemade bread spread with jam—but I was anxious to start back. Aunt Minnie gave me a jar of raspberry jam to take to Mother and walked with me to the dam. Great bushes of yellow and orange jewel weed grew at one spot near the water. I started to pick some, but Aunt Minnie held my arm and pointed. A ruby-throated hummingbird was thrusting his needle-like bill into one blossom after another. His green feathers gleamed in the sun, and his red throat feathers were ruffled. He moved his wings so fast that I could scarcely see them.

A few minutes later, feeling rested and ready for the row down the lake, I started off again. Aunt Minnie lifted her cane and waved. I waved back and as I rowed by the tall rushes, I looked hard for a heron. This was the kind of spot he loved, and sure enough I saw one standing motionless on one leg, his gray-blue color blending into the gray of an old log. He didn't move until I got very near and then he rose soundlessly, flapping his great, wide wings and dragging his long, thin legs.

I kept close to the shore opposite the one I had followed in the morning. There were not so many coves, and so it was shorter. The banks were steep and high; pines and hemlocks grew at the water's edge and I rowed in their dark shadows. A little chipmunk sat on a granite boulder at the edge of the water and scolded me, and a little beyond that I found the best prize of all for my treasure box. It was a luna moth that had fallen into the water. Its pale green wings were the most delicate color I had ever seen. Each wing narrowed to a graceful tail, and the protective spots in the middle of each wing were a rich purple. I picked it up carefully, feeling sad to realize how short its life had been.

The wind was with me and I was rowing easily as I turned the corner into our part of the lake. I could see the tall pine by our boathouse in the distance, and in a short time I reached the pond-lily cove. I had spent many hours here with Uncle Lon, and while he fished, I had learned the cove by heart. There was the tall half-dead maple tree where a king-fisher always sat. One small live branch at the top of the tree waved some crimson leaves long before frost time. Just below the surface was the submerged log of a giant tree much bigger than any standing on the shore, and there was the little strip of sand where sandpipers ran up and down on their match-thin legs and traced a fine pattern with their tiny feet. I picked a few lilies, taking care to break their long stems way down at the bottom. I curled them round and round and laid them in the shade under the seat. Their fragrance was all around me, mixed with the smell of water-soaked logs.

Home was very near now. I thought I could see Susan across the water, standing by our float ready for a swim.

It was a half mile across the middle of the lake and I had promised not to cross it, so I rowed on close to the shore, feeling impatient now, but beginning also to have a feeling of triumph. Finally, I cut across the narrow end of the lake by the bridge, and just before reaching the boathouse I stopped, with the oars dragging in the water. I wanted to keep this day all to myself for a few more minutes. I was wrapped around with a scarf of blue sky and silver water, of wind and strange, new feelings.

Then I gave the call of the loon, "Who-o-o, who-o-o." Way off up the lake came a faint answer—but I knew the mother loon would never again let me get near her babies.

FIVE

The Store and Peddlers

In Saco it was easy to walk down the street to the grocer's, or the fish market, or the bakery. If Mother wanted a spool of thread or a yard of cloth, Miss Barber's dry goods store was not very far away. But in Waterboro Center it was quite different; the only sources of supply were Marsh Cousens' store and the peddlers who came by once in a while.

I liked to go to the store to do the errands. It was down the road a very short distance and faced Grandfather's field. It had been painted yellow once, but most of the paint was worn off and there was no paint at all on the gray boards of the uncovered porch in front. At one end of the porch were some iron platform scales which were big enough to

64

weigh large sacks of potatoes or grain. At the other end there was a long seat made by one wide board fastened roughly to the side of the building. Three or four overturned nail kegs nearby could also be used for seats.

The postoffice was in the store and men would gather on the porch a half hour before the stage was due, whether they expected mail or not, and exchange opinions about the weather and crops. These were very important subjects to farmers, and women and children who didn't have knowledge about such things never interrupted.

Marsh Cousens, the storekeeper, was a thin, lanky man with a lot of untidy gray hair and a walrus mustache that drooped way down on one side, but looked as if he had chewed it off on the other side. He wore wide suspenders and kept the sleeves of his shirt up with ordinary elastics which he snapped now and then when they felt tight. He wore a stiff straw hat whether he was outside or inside the store, and I knew it was the same hat year after year because there was a break between the crown and the rim and sometimes a little tuft of grayish hair stuck through the hole. If someone bought stamps to send away in a letter, Marsh would take off his hat and rub the glue side of the stamps on his hair. This, he claimed, was the way to keep them from sticking together. He was one of the few grownups that we children called by his first name. Maybe we did this because he didn't seem to have any age and maybe because everyone in the village, young and old, called him "Marsh."

The store was open by six in the morning every day of the week except Sunday and on Sunday it was open by eight o'clock. Marsh kept it open in the evening as long as anyone would hang around to talk or play checkers. The checkerboard was always waiting on top of a barrel at the back of the store. He lived alone upstairs. Somehow I never wondered if he had relatives. He just belonged to the store.

Directly inside the door of the store on the left was the enclosure for the postoffice. It was easy to look through the glass of the boxes and sometimes I saw Marsh in there, sitting on a high stool and reading someone's newspaper that had not been called for.

Next to the postoffice was the glass case for the penny candy. While Marsh was getting my purchase, I liked to look it over carefully and think about what I might buy when I had some pennies of my own. On the floor, beneath the candy case, was a box filled with bottles of Moxie, a strange half-sweet, half-bitter drink that was fun to have just because I couldn't guess what was in it.

The long counter next to the candy case was high and black. It must have been painted once but it had received hard wear for many years and was marked with cuts from the big knife Marsh used on a number of things. He would reach behind the counter into the earthen crock that held salty brine, pull out a long, narrow piece of salt pork and slice off the required amount onto the counter. Or he would uncover the big cartwheel of well-seasoned cheese, lift it from its box and neatly cut off an exact pound, but always in such a way that a thin sliver was left on the knife. He would then hold out the knife to me and I would break off half of the little sliver of cheese and say "thank you" and he would pop the other small piece into his own mouth.

On the shelves behind the counter were spices—whole cloves, round nutmegs the size of marbles which Mother had to rub against a special grater to get off the small, pungent grains, and dark brown, tightly curled cinnamon bark in a glass jar. There was also a jar of flaxseed which was used to make poultices. On the top shelf stood a row of thin glass chimneys and a heap of the wicks for the kerosene lamps everyone used. On another shelf was yellow flypaper in sticky rectangular sheets and round narrow rolls. Marsh had several of these rolls hanging from the ceiling of the store.

Under the counter was a barrel of flour and a barrel of sugar which was weighed out in a large metal scale pan on some scales at the far end of the counter. Marsh had three cats and sometimes one of them would be found cozily curled up in the scale pan. Marsh would gently lower the pan to the floor, tip the cat out and then vigorously bang the scale pan against his knee. It was his way of cleaning it.

Several times I went to the store in the early morning and found all three cats on the counter eating salmon which Marsh had emptied from a can. "Hadn't ought to do this," he would say, stroking one of the cats till it arched its back and purred "These cats are getting too fat to catch the mice," but he tipped out more salmon just the same. Grandfather once said the cats were Marsh's children.

On the right side of the store was a second counter and on this was the big red coffee grinder and long pieces of dark brown plug tobacco which were creased to mark off where they were to be cut. A box of white clay pipes was on the same counter. They cost one cent each and Susan and I liked to buy them to use for blowing soap bubbles. Another box was full of fish hooks of three or four sizes. Since I never owned more than two fish hooks at a time and was always tearing them off in the alderbushes or on a rock in the lake, I looked at this box with special interest.

Standing on the floor and leaning against the counter were big open gunny sacks full of beans—pea beans, yellow eye beans, kidney beans. I liked to put my hand into a bag and feel the beans slip smoothly between my fingers.

At the back of the store were several barrels. One held the round common crackers that were so good in chowder. Another was full of big cucumber pickles floating in vinegar and water. If somebody wanted one he stuck his hand in the liquid and picked it out. The pickles cost a cent each.

Two of the barrels were in wooden cradles and were lying on their sides. Each had a spigot in the end. In one was vinegar and in the other molasses. Grandfather made our vinegar from our own apples by putting some of the brown substance called "mother" into a barrel of cider and letting it stand for a year, but we often bought molasses. Gingerbread was our favorite dessert and molasses was delicious on oatmeal. Our brown earthenware jug held just a gallon of molasses and Marsh would let the slow stream of rich, brown molasses flow into the jug until, all of a sudden, it was ready to overflow. Sometimes, I put my hand out to catch the last drop hanging on the spigot and then I licked my fingers. In this part of the store, too, was the large metal can of kerosene from which Marsh filled the smaller can that I brought over from the house. There was a dark spot on the floor where some of the kerosene had dripped and the odor of the store was a blend of kerosene, and cheese and leather and people.

There was a big, open wooden box by the back window and lying on it was a pile of seven or eight dried codfish. They didn't look good at all, but when Mother soaked one of these fish for an hour or more and cooked it in cream sauce and mixed it with hard boiled eggs and potatoes, we thought it was delicious.

Marsh did not carry fresh meat. There was no way to keep it from spoiling, so we were very glad that Mr. Warren Day came to the house nearly every week. When his small, brown horse pulled up to the side door and we heard a long, drawn-out "Whoa," Susan and I followed Mother outside and watched while she made her selections. He had a large black box the size of a steamer trunk on the back of the cart and a heavy horse blanket was thrown over it so that the ice inside would not melt. He did his own butchering and Mother and Grandfather thought his meat was better than any in the Saco store. I guess he thought of us as special customers because we ate some kinds of meat no one else wanted. He charged us ten cents for calves' liver in order to get rid of it and gave us the sweetbreads instead of feeding them to his dog.

One time Mother said she would like to try cooking calves' brains. When Mr. Day came the next week, he handed Mother a paper bag and said it was the calf's brain. That morning without opening the bag, Mother spent some time reading the cookbook. I was putting away the breakfast dishes in the dining room cupboard when I heard her give a little gasp, as if she had hurt herself. I could see that her face was very white and I started to call Grandfather. She was twisting the top of the paper bag shut. "Don't come in here, children," she said. "Stay away. I have to bury this bag and I don't want you to come with me." Susan and I looked at each other uncertainly and then we heard Mother get the shovel in the barn and go out.

Grandfather was curious by now and when Mother came back he wanted to know what the fuss was about. Mother put her hand to her eyes. "That was the whole head of a calf," she said. "Its eyes were looking right at me." It was a long time before she could speak of it again. Fortunately, Mr. Day was a quiet man and did not ask her about it.

It took a lot of planning, not only to get food, but to keep it. We had no ice. We kept perishable food down in the cool cellar. Halfway down the cellar stairs were shelves for the jugs of vinegar and molasses. The floor of the cellar was brick and the walls were sheathed in brick. In the center of the floor was a big table and over it was a hanging shelf. After each meal Susan and I took turns carrying the food downstairs and placing it on the table or shelf. Then we put a dome-shaped wire mesh cover over each dish just in case some flies were about.

Our milk came from the Stewarts' farm nearby. Each morning Susan and I walked over there carrying empty tin milk cans. We left the empty cans with Mrs. Stewart and brought back the ones she had filled from the milking of the night before. The cellar floor was cool and we stood the milk cans on it.

Once or twice a summer Grandfather had a bunch of bananas sent out from Portland and brought up by the stage. A bunch of bananas cost about a dollar and a quarter. They were very green when they arrived but, after hanging a week in the cellar, they became yellow and delicious.

Mother loved to experiment and, though the calf's brain was a failure, she did have good luck in another way. This was in making soap. Every summer she saved the fat from cooking meat like beef and roast lamb and stored it in big lard pails down cellar. Then toward the end of our vacation in Waterboro she made soap. First she filled a large kettle with the fat and slowly melted it down on the back of the kitchen stove. Sometimes it had a pretty strong smell so she did this when she could keep the outer kitchen door open. When the liquid fat had been strained and she had added the borax and lye, the soap was ready to pour into a large wooden box which she had lined with white cloth from an old pillow-case.

This kind of soap was only good for washing clothes, although it looked fine grained and was a pale yellow color. It was put away in the attic to ripen over the winter but still it was too strong and hurt our hands. But one summer Mother decided she should be able to make some really nice soap. She read that adding cucumbers would make it a finer quality so she sent me out in the garden to get some big, over-ripe cucumbers and she put these in the soap with green dye and rosewater. The result was a little too soft, but much better than the earlier soap and she was proud of it. We children were not allowed to have any part in this process for fear the lye would get on us and burn us.

When we left Saco and came to Waterboro, Mother tried to bring with her a good supply of sewing materials, because there was no place nearby where she could buy cloth or hooks and eyes. Marsh Cousens did have one box of Corticelli sewing silk. It was made of highly polished light wood and there was a picture of a kitten on the top. In it were about ten narrow drawers filled with rows of sewing silk. He also carried a box of heavy white thread and one of black thread.

Mother was glad, as were all the women in the village, when the notion wagon came to Waterboro Center. The good-natured driver, whose name was Louis, drove his high, green van up to the Tompkins place once every summer. He planned to spend the night there and, while he was unhitching his two sturdy horses, the news spread around that he was there. His coming was a real event in our village. Many women didn't get to a city store more than once a year and some not at all.

Louis' plan was to stop in a central spot and then move on to another spot where there was a group of houses. The women within walking distance came to him. He must have decided that they would buy more when several of them were looking at his stock together. Among the few single houses he went to was the Newcombs because the Newcomb sisters were too shy to let other women see their purchases. He didn't stop at our house but when he came to the Tompkinses' Mother walked down there and if Susan and I were around we happily went along too.

Usually my interest in the notion wagon had little to do with Mother's purchases, but it was such an amazing van with big drawers along the side and little drawers at the back and several doors in unexpected places that I hoped I could be on hand when Louis opened it up.

Louis seemed to carry as much as Miss Barber's dry goods store in Saco. He unrolled bolts of calico and gingham, talking so pleasantly all the time that the women soon were smiling and eager to see more. He had everything from corset strings and Hamburg trimming to yard goods and flowers to trim hats. If someone started to edge away, he noticed it at once and picked up a piece of cloth and held it next to the woman's face, telling her it was just the thing to match her pretty eyes.

We children watched him and listened a little shyly to his jokes, but when he came over to us and showed Mother some pretty green ribbon, she bought us each new hair ribbons, though she had not planned to at all.

One time Louis came to Waterboro on a Saturday afternoon and that evening there was to be a square dance in the town hall, an event which occurred every few weeks in the summer. The doors and windows of the hall were usually wide open and if the wind was just right Susan and I, lying in bed, could faintly hear the music of the fiddle. Later in the night when I had been asleep a long time, I might be roused by the sound of carriages going by the house. The horses would be trotting fast so that the wheels made a loud crunching noise on the pebbles in the dirt road and people would be calling happily to one another.

73

On this particular Saturday night, Louis was staying as usual at the Tompkinses' and Mary Tompkins asked him if he would like to go with her to the dance. I was in the black-smith shop the next morning when Mary came over to tell Mr. Sawyer, the blacksmith, about it. The peddler had danced so well and had been so gay that all the girls had a wonderful time with him and several were coming this morning to make purchases from his notion wagon.

There was another peddler who came through our village just once, but I could never forget him. He was small and dried up, with black hair and a very white face. He was walking and wheeling a baby carriage filled with shoestrings and spools of thread. He must have walked a long way and the thread didn't look very clean.

Grandfather came to the door when he knocked and said curtly that we didn't need anything. Mother was standing right behind him and quickly said she needed some shoe-laces. The man's sad face looked a little happier as Mother bought several things. Then Mother stepped inside and told Grandfather she was going to ask the peddler to dinner. Grandfather protested that we might catch something from him but Mother didn't listen to a word. I had never seen her more aroused. She quickly filled a plate with the fricassee chicken we were having for dinner and covered a pile of mashed potatoes with a lot of gravy. She cut out a big piece of blueberry pie and poured a glass of milk. Then she put all this dinner on a tray and quickly carried it out to the side steps. I followed her out and watched. I had never before seen a very hungry person eat.

74

SIX

The Mail Stage

Waterboro Center's most important daily event was the passing of the mail stage. We had dinner before the afternoon stage went down. We went in swimming after the stage came up. We decided when we would do many things by the coming and going of the stage. Its first trip started ten miles north of our village in Limerick and after stopping at North Waterboro and at mailboxes beside the road it reached Marsh Cousens' store at seven o'clock in the morning.

Len Doughty was the driver and he had a long open wagon with two crosswise seats for passengers and plenty of space behind for bags of mail and freight. Len drove two horses, one gray and one brown, and they usually trotted up to the store as if they knew they were on important business. Marsh would be waiting for the stage and would fling in the mailbag so that Len could drive right along, unless he had to take on passengers. The stage had to reach East Waterboro in time for the mail to be sorted and put on the trains for Portland and Boston.

By nine o'clock Len was back, bringing our mail and the Boston paper. He could stop now and come into the store because the mailbag had to be opened and the mail for our village taken out. Grandfather liked to be on hand for the sorting because Len had time to tell all the news about the families up and down his route. There were many things Grandfather and the neighbors wanted to know, like whether the water was going over the dam at the other end of the lake and whether the smelts were still running in the smelt stream and who was doing the Widow Hobbs' haying for her. If I had finished wiping the breakfast dishes and had made my bed, I usually walked over with Grandfather; and then, if he felt he must stay longer to talk things over, he would sit down on one of the nail kegs on the store porch and send me back to the house with the mail. I noticed that the men standing around seemed anxious to get Grandfather's opinion on what was happening in Augusta. Grandfather had been in the state legislature when he was younger.

At one-thirty Len was back with the afternoon stage. He just had time to eat his dinner in Limerick and start back to East Waterboro on his second trip. He drove a fresh pair of horses and they were better looking than the morning pair. They were both black. Len sometimes had his shirt collar buttoned up and his hat on for these afternoon trips because he might have passengers to bring up from the Portland and Boston trains. Often, when Aunt Lu and Aunt Addie were coming to see us, they rode on this afternoon stage.

Len was a tall, thin man with a comical face. He looked as if he were always smiling even when he wasn't at all. He liked children and never failed to wave to the boys and girls he happened to pass. He drove hunched way over so that it was quite a surprise when he uncurled and swung himself to the ground and we could see what Grandfather meant when he called Len "as tall as a lamppost." The horses knew the route so well that Len held the reins loosely and the horses pulled up to the store and stopped without a word from him.

I liked to say "Hello" to Len on this second trip. There were not many people around then because the farmers had mostly gone to the fields for haying or were busy in their gardens or barnyards. Len sometimes told me about his niece and nephew who lived near the other end of the lake. Their names were Agnes and John. He pretended they could catch much bigger perch than I could but, after telling me about them, he would give a big wink and I was pretty sure he was fooling me.

There was one time in the year when Len made his team look especially nice and that was the Fourth of July. The stage did not carry mail on the Fourth but Len made the morning trip in order to bring up the newspapers. He used the black horses and he tied red, white and blue ribbons on their harnesses and a ribbon on the whip. One Fourth he drove Mr. Andrews' old colonial coach that had not been used for fifty years. He oiled its springs and tested it out carefully. The day before the Fourth he told Susan and me he was going to drive the coach and he wanted all the children along the way to wave their flags as he went by. I sat on the top rail of Grandfather's fence and waved with all my might as he came along.

Len was very clever with tools and he did a lot of odd jobs besides driving the stage. Most of the farmhouses in Limerick and Waterboro got their water from pumps. There were a few wells, of course, but these were not convenient in cold weather. The point on an iron pipe was driven deep into the ground in the cellar and the water was then drawn up into the kitchen sink by a hand pump. If the pump brought up very little water it was often because the suction was not strong and Len would be sent for to put a new leather collar inside the pump. When he fixed our pump, I thought the leather made the water taste queer and it certainly took more strength to push the pump handle down, but Len laughed at me and said if I would just pump twenty-five strokes I could get a delicious cold drink from the northeast corner of the well.

Len was also clever at fixing clocks and that meant a great deal to people in the country. As he drove back and forth with the mail, he was stopped from time to time by someone whose clock would not go. Len would jump out, twisting the reins around the whipstock, and would run into the farmhouse to look at the clock. They said at the store he could make a clock go by squirting a little sewing machine oil into it and shaking it just right, but when other people tried the same method it did not work. If he had passengers in the stage when he was called on to fix a clock, he would promise to return in a minute, but occasionally he was gone quite a while. Then he would have to urge the horses to trot faster to make up the time. Grandfather thought mail and clocks should not mix.

Occasionally Len carried the works of a clock in a box under his seat, and while he waited for mail to be sorted, he might pull them out and start looking over all the little wheels. One time he was almost late with the mail because of his interest in machinery. In Limerick there was a man named Mr. Higgins who owned a Stanley Steamer. It was a wonderful machine and one of the first automobiles we had ever seen. When we heard it coming, Susan and I often ran to the fence in front of our house to watch it go by in a cloud of dust.

I heard Len say in the store, one day, that if he just had a machine like that, he could take the mail through in no time and would never be delayed. Marsh Cousens thought maybe Len was saving his clock money to buy an automobile. Then someone from Limerick told Grandfather that Len was talking of selling the black horses. We could hardly believe it.

A little later Len was way behind time with the one-thirty stage. He had never been late enough to miss getting the mail to the trains and Grandfather was quite upset, but just at the last minute Len drove up. His horses looked as if they had been running hard.

"Been fixing clocks?" Grandfather asked crossly.

"No," Len said as he reached for the mailbag. "No, Mr.

Higgins is stuck two miles up the road. I thought maybe I could help him, but I couldn't do a dang thing." Then as he picked up the reins he added, "I guess you can count on horses better than machines for carrying the mail."

Once a summer, Mother took Susan and me to Portland for the day and we had to get up very early to catch the first stage. Grandfather didn't see any use in hitching up Nellie and driving the two miles to the station when Len charged only twenty-five cents a person between the store and the station.

The early morning dew and the little silvery spider webs were on the grass as we walked carefully in our best shoes over to the store. A soft line of gray mist was hanging just above the ground in the distant part of Grandfather's field, but just a few feet above it the day was shining.

We loved the ride behind Len's two horses, even if they were the unmatched pair. They trotted most of the way and they seemed to be going very fast. Len never touched them with his whip but now and then, as he left a mailbox, he would give a loud crack of the whip in the air. Len whistled softly a good part of the way. He had to stop at a number of mailboxes and when he looked carefully over the mail he picked up, some of it made him whistle louder.

It was cold at that hour before the sun had dried the fields, but we knew it would be hot on our return so we didn't take coats; instead we snuggled down under a robe.

The first stop was at the Warrens' which was just opposite Grandfather's woods. Len said there was usually a fat envelope in the box. Mrs. Warren sold Larkin's soap and sent her orders in by mail. A few times I had walked down as far as her house to buy fresh eggs for Mother. Mrs. Warren had taken me into her parlor and shown me the many pieces of furniture she had bought with soap coupons. It seemed like a wonderful way to get pretty things for nothing.

Halfway to the station was Roberts' pickle factory, a small gray building where delicious cucumber pickles were made. Mother thought the sandy soil of Waterboro grew the best cucumbers anywhere. The smell of the vinegar tickled our noses as we stopped, and Len lifted up two barrels of pickles to go by freight to Portland.

Len left us on the station platform with a quick wave of his hand and a friendly twitch to my braids, and drove over to the East Waterboro store and postoffice across the way.

I didn't like these summer trips to Portland very much. The train had come from Boston and the car was hot and stuffy. Susan and I both felt carsick and when Mother opened the window the cinders and smoke from the engine made us feel worse. There was a thin layer of cinders on the window-sill and we couldn't help getting the sleeves of our clean dresses dirty as we leaned against the window in the hope of breathing fresh air.

The ride in the open trolley car from the Portland station up to the big stores revived us. We walked along the brick sidewalks looking into the big store windows. The streets, which were paved with cobblestones, seemed full of horses and wagons, with a few carriages and one or two automobiles among them. The purpose of our trip was to buy things for the opening of school and first we were fitted to school boots and then Mother bought cloth for school dresses.

Every fall Mother sent to Best & Co. for a special sailor suit and a coat for each of us, but all our other clothes, as well as Mother's dresses, were made by a dressmaker, Mrs. Guptill. She came to the house in Saco for a week at a time. Mother also made dresses for us, though she found this hard to do. Sometimes, when she bought some particularly pretty material, she would decide to work with it herself and would buy enough for a dress for Susan or me. Then she would spend hours cutting it out on the dining-room table, and I would have to stand still for a very long time while she tried it on and fitted it to me.

I was a thoughtless little girl, though I didn't mean to be. Once Mother made me a pink Indianhead sailor suit trimmed with white braid. It took her a long time to make it and I liked it very much. The second time I wore it I went to a birthday party in Saco and played hide-and-seek with the other children. I caught my new dress on a picket fence and tore a jagged hole in the back of the skirt. Mother was more sad than angry. She didn't understand why I had to go over the fence instead of around.

On our Portland trip, besides cloth, Mother bought us new hair ribbons, red ones and dark blue ones for school, and pale pink ones for me and light blue ones for Susan. These last were to wear to dancing school. The ribbon counter with its rolls and rolls of lovely wide ribbon filled me with a tingling delight. I decided I would love to own a small piece of each ribbon and keep them in a box just to look at, never to wear.

They made me think of the dry goods store in Saco where there were spools of "baby ribbon" hanging behind the counter. The ribbon was rolled down from the spools for six or seven inches and sometimes the colors were tangled together. The ribbon was only a quarter of an inch wide and curled around as it hung. It cost two cents a yard and was mostly used to run through insertion on corset covers. If I could get by the candy store next door, I sometimes invested in a half yard of some lovely color and I threaded the ribbon through a little booklet of verses I had copied for Mother. But I could never hope to own the wide, expensive ribbons in the Portland store.

After a while, the Portland sidewalks began to feel awfully hard to Susan and me. We had been running around the fields of Waterboro in sneakers and our shoes felt tight. We were glad when Mother said we had time for some ice cream and a trolley ride. We went first into Lord's store and had a dish of delicious chocolate ice cream. In the ceiling were fans with wide mahogany blades that looked like canoe paddles. They whirled around slowly cooling us off after our busy shopping and blowing toward us the sweet smell of caramels and ice cream. The small tables had smooth white marble tops and twisting iron legs. We chose to sit in the corner where there was a long comfortable seat of cool slippery leather, and where the mirrors on both walls reflected the ice cream counter and the show case filled with candy.

When we left Lord's we climbed into an open trolley car which went up Munjoy Hill to Fort Allen Park. We sat on the front seat of the trolley and the breeze blew around us. The trolley stopped opposite the park for five minutes before returning to the center of the city, so we jumped out and looked at the blue ocean stretching out between the green islands to the open sea. Just below us a six-masted schooner was anchored and at least twenty schooners with two or three masts were either anchored or getting their sails ready for leaving. A little beyond them, a four-masted schooner with all its white sails set was moving away from the shore. Was it going to China, perhaps? Mother said it might be.

But for all the excitement of the day, it was good to arrive once more at the East Waterboro station, to smell the pines and to see the outline of our mountain. We were on the late train so Len was not there, but Grandfather and Nellie were waiting.

I knew that Len who was full of jokes, would probably tease me the next day when I came over with Grandfather for the first mail. "So you didn't come back in time to ride up with me," he said. "I suppose I drive too slow." His eyes twinkled and we both laughed. I hoped that some day I could ride all the way to Limerick in his fast stage.

SEVEN

A Walk up the Mountain

A walk up the mountain was an adventure. Every summer we waited for the perfect day, not too hot for a walk of four miles, and with clear air so that we could see plainly the White Mountains in New Hampshire. One morning at breakfast Mother said, "I think we could see Mount Washington if we climbed the mountain today." That was all Susan and I needed to start getting ready. Grandfather, who had been reading the *Farmers' Almanac*, was a little doubtful. He thought that the few big, fluffy white clouds that were in the sky over the back field might join together and make a thunderstorm, but his doubts didn't disturb us.

While Mother made sandwiches, Susan and I got together

tin cups and baskets to hold blueberries. We tied our sweaters by the sleeves around our waists, even though it was a warm day, and I hunted up a long stick in the woodshed. We would put it through the handles of the picnic basket and Susan and I would divide the weight by holding opposite ends. This plan usually did not last for long because the basket slid from one side to the other when we failed to keep the stick level.

Mother got her cane from the back hall. It was the top of an Alpine staff that she had brought home from Europe years ago. She walked so lightly and easily that she did not use it for support, but she enjoyed carrying it on a long walk. Mother was wearing a long, blue linen skirt that came below the tops of her black lace boots. Her white shirtwaist buttoned down the back and a rather wide hat of rough straw kept the sun off her face. We children had on gingham dresses that were a little tight and hot but the skirts were pleated and walking was easy in our sneakers. Grandfather was in his garden as we started. I waved to him and he gave one of his quick nods.

The road was sandy and crossed the marshy end of the lake a little distance from our house. We had not started to go uphill and were not in need of a rest when we reached this spot, but we always stopped and put behind us, in our thoughts, all the duties and play activities back at the house. Here was the open door to our day.

There was a big granite boulder by the water and room for all three of us to sit and look down into a shallow pool. We saw little, dark minnows in frightened crowds darting away from a hungry perch. They never seemed to divide and scatter but kept in a tight bunch and maybe this frightened the big fish chasing them. Small black water bugs that looked like beetles made twisting patterns on the surface of the water and a thin water spider skated along without sinking in at all.

Since the lake ended here, the water was full of tall rushes and red-winged blackbirds were churring and swaying in them. On several logs that were partly out of the water mud turtles were sunning themselves. Some of them slipped off— plop, plop. The big bullfrogs stopped their deep "kerchug" as we walked near. I thought if I tiptoed I could see one before he stopped giving me the right direction, but though I looked very carefully I could not find the big frogs. When I walked on the grass near the edge of the water, three or four very little frogs jumped into the water in a high arc and I could see them swimming away. They disappeared under the jelly-like stuff that mother called mosquito eggs.

Dragonflies hovered over the lily pads. There were big black ones that moved so fast that their gauzy wings were almost invisible. Occasionally, one would seem to stop perfectly still in the air, a trick which seemed impossible, and then it would suddenly dart away in a straight line. There were other shorter, smaller dragonflies with bright blue bodies. We had been told by Aunt Addie that dragonflies are called "darning needles" and that they sew up the mouths of people who tell fibs. Though we children knew they really could not sew up our mouths, we didn't quite like to have them light on us.

There were some especially large, beautiful water lilies a

short distance from the shore. Since no boat could be used in this marshy part of the lake, there was no way to reach them. I asked Mother if I couldn't come in my bathing suit someday and swim out to the lilies but she said I must never do that. People who had too many kittens drowned them in this part of the lake and the water was not clean.

As we left the lake the road went into the woods. Alderbushes and ferns crowded into the road, but behind them were the pines and they shaded us as we walked along. On our left was a stone wall which ran up the hill for some distance and in many places was completely hidden by bushes. Grandfather had told us that this was the old Carl place. There were two girls in the Carl family who had married very rich men in Chicago. They came back to Waterboro Center once in a great while to visit the cemetery behind the town hall and they had paid part of the cost of the new cemetery wall.

As we walked along we came to a spot where there once had been a gate leading into the Carl place. We climbed through and went in under the big trees. This was our second stop. There was no trace of the house that had been here at the time of the Civil War but there were two very old apple trees that looked out of place among the pines.

It was very quiet. We sat down on the trunk of a fallen hemlock. Trailing on the ground around our feet grew prince's pine. The pale yellow spikes that stood up straight out of the green vines looked like tiny candles. We kept still while Mother whistled softly and the shy little warblers and friendly chickadees lighted nearby. The mosquitoes came too so we each picked a frond of a long fern and waved them around our heads as we went back to the road.

The Frost farm was the halfway point on our walk up the mountain and we always sat down in the grass by the gate. There were quantities of checkerberries here and Susan and I started to pick the short stalks with their bronze leaves and bright red berries, but all at once we realized that Grandfather had been right about a thunderstorm. Big, black clouds were piling up in the sky. On the opposite side of the road from the farm were some very tall white pines. Grandfather had once said that this woodlot was the oldest in Waterboro and had not been cut for a hundred years. These trees had hidden the approaching storm.

On the farmhouse side of the road, the forest had been cleared away many years before and there was an apple orchard. Through this we could see the small red house and the big, unpainted barn of Isaiah and Josiah Frost. But we didn't dare go into the yard because somewhere in there was a terrifying black dog that barked furiously.

Always, on a walk up the mountain, I looked eagerly to see if one of the Frost brothers was in sight. If Isaiah was working in his garden, he might straighten up and lean on his hoe as we stood by the gate but he would only nod briefly if I called, "Hello, Mr. Frost." He did not ask us to come in.

It was quite different if Josiah was around. He was a short, jolly little man with bushy white hair and red cheeks—a contrast to his tall, thin brother whose straggly beard was unnaturally black for his age. The brothers lived alone and Isaiah never left the farm, but Josiah liked to come down to the village to sell his eggs and to talk with the men at Marsh Cousens' store.

Under one of the apple trees inside the gate of their farm was a spring of delicious, cold water. It welled up from clean white sand with little crystal bubbles and around it grew mint and catnip. If Josiah saw us by his gate he would call, "Come in, come in. Have a drink." We always stepped in gratefully, knowing the dog would be friendly if Josiah spoke to him. We drank from a tin cup left on a rock by the spring and the smell of the crushed mint as we knelt seemed to give the water a wonderful flavor.

Now, as the thunderstorm drew nearer, Mother wondered what we should do. Perhaps we could find some shelter among the big pines or maybe the dog would not harm us if we went to the door of the Frost farm and asked if we could wait in the barn till the shower passed over. We were thankful when we heard Josiah calling, "Come in, now jest step into the kitchen until this rain is gone. It won't do ye a mite of good to go in them woods."

We hurried through the orchard to the house and barely got inside when the big drops began to fall. We had never been in the house before, and we tried to look around without seeming too curious. The kitchen floor was unpainted, but the wide, bare boards had been scrubbed so hard and so often that they had a slippery sheen. The floor was uneven in some spots as if it had been worn down by years of walking. There was a wooden table against the wall and that, too, was unpainted and worn. There were two straight split-bottom chairs. Their deep sumac-red stain showed they had been made by the Shakers. The storm made the room very dark, but we could see a large, black wood-burning stove and an iron sink with a window above it. There were no curtains or rugs, and the walls had become dark with wood smoke.

Mother sat down, but we children stood by the door watching the storm. It gradually grew lighter and I looked over by the door leading to another room. I could see a big drum standing by the wall and, without thinking much, I went over and touched it. The deep, rich vibration surprised me, but I was more startled when the bedroom door was thrown violently open. "Don't touch that drum!" Isaiah Frost shouted.

"No harm done," Josiah said.

Isaiah glared at him and picked up the drum. But before he could carry it into the bedroom, Mother said, "What a beautiful drum! Can either of you play it?"

Isaiah straightened up and threw his head back so that he looked very tall. "Play it, ma'am! Why, I was a drummer boy twelve years old in the Mexican War, and I beat this drum ahead of General Scott going into Mexico City."

We looked at him with astonishment, and then Mother said softly, "How proud you must be! You would do us a great favor if you would play for us."

Josiah didn't say a word, and we all waited, holding our breath. Isaiah hesitated for a moment, then he put the broad leather strap around his neck and picked up the drumsticks. He took a faded cap from a peg beside the door and put it on. We realized it was a soldier's hat. He moved over to the window and I could see his pale blue eyes were looking far away into the distance. Then, suddenly, the roll of the drum filled the room. It was not a simple rat-tat-tat, but was like the peal of thunder—now distant, now right at hand. It was the sound of horses' hoofs and of soldiers' feet marching, marching, and behind it the vigor of a young man.

He stopped as suddenly as he had begun, and when we said, "Oh, thank you very, very much," Isaiah's severe face broke into a half smile. "Come again," he said and walked quickly into the other room.

The storm was soon over and Josiah walked with us to the gate. He hadn't said a word, and we realized he was as surprised as we were by his brother's words. At the gate, he seemed to be echoing Isaiah as he said, "Come again!"

Water was running down the hill in little brooks on both sides of the road. But the center of the sandy road was dry, and we decided to go on to the top of our mountain. As we started up the road we looked back at the house and saw Isaiah standing in the door. He raised his hand to his forehead in a military salute.

The sun was shining and a brisk breeze was shaking the raindrops off the trees and blowing all the clouds away. It would be clear when we reached the top of the mountain and we went happily on our way.

We came to a very steep hill and we walked resolutely up it, stopping once in the middle to catch our breath and to look back at a small silver piece of our lake that showed through the trees. At the top of this hill was a level stretch and in the middle of the road five or six swallowtail butterflies were drying their wings. The pale yellow of their wings was outlined with black dots and they fanned them back and forth in the sun. Several orange-and-black monarch butterflies were on the sweet milkweed blossoms by the side of the road. We remembered how, once, we had sat on a flat rock at this spot and watched a monarch butterfly slowly come out of its cocoon which was attached to a nearby boulder. When its wings were dry, it flew away and Mother said it was a miracle.

At this point we left the road which went over a ridge toward Rosses' Corner and took a footpath through the woods. The big pine trees had thinned out and the sun shone through the birches and poplars, making yellow patterns on the leafy path. We did not stop because now we were eager to reach the top and see the view. Soon we stepped out on a great rock. Wind and storms had smoothed off the sharp edges of the granite ledge. There was one shallow depression in the middle which was filled with rain from the recent storm and on the sheltered side thin slivers of isinglass shone in the sun. A few red columbines pressed against the rock for protection.

I stood up straight, happy to have come so far, and the breeze blew through my clothes, cooling me off. I could see our village and the lake below. I thought our farm looked like a little dollhouse and I imagined I could see Grandfather in his garden. I found the store, the blacksmith shop, and the town hall, and Susan and I called to Mother, "Look, look!" as Len Doughty's stage drew up to the store. Our lake was like a piece of lovely blue silk among the green trees. To my surprise I could see a black squall moving across the water from one shore to the other. It was wonderful to watch it from this height instead of being in a boat and dreading the swift approach of that black line of water.

We had not reached the very top of the mountain. From this ledge we could only see in one direction and we recognized our own familiar landmarks. We found delight in fitting it into a pattern, like a jigsaw puzzle, and in realizing that our village was part of a bigger picture that included, way in the distance, a thin silver line that was Lake Sebago. Just possibly the spot on the horizon where the blue seemed more intense was the ocean, and Mother thought a faraway faint column of smoke came from a factory chimney in Portland.

Another reason for stopping on the ledge before finishing our climb was the fact that Howard Elsworth lived nearby. His house was just under the crest of the mountain, a low building black with age. Mr. Elsworth was a real hermit. He had a long, gray beard that came down almost to his waist and his voice was a slow singsong. Mother suggested he must talk to himself and that he imitated the soft sound of the wind in the pines. We knew him well. He walked down to the store every few weeks and usually stopped by to sell us blueberries. He claimed that the biggest and sweetest blueberries to be found grew on the sunny slope behind his house. To prove it he once brought down short sprays broken from the bushes. They were so heavy with the juicy round berries that they bent way over. Mother put them in an old blue sugar bowl on the dining-room table and we children gradually ate off the delicious fruit.

We had only been on the ledge a few minutes when Mr. Elsworth came out to join us, bringing his telescope with him. Years earlier the Coast Guard had a station on our mountain because it was the first point of land that sailors coming into Portland Harbor could see. But Mount Agamenticus was nearer the sea and finally the Coast Guard moved there. Mr. Elsworth was given a telescope when they left. He claimed it was very powerful, but when I held it to my eyes I couldn't see a thing. It wobbled around and first a black patch, then a very large leaf and then a strange piece of the woods moved swiftly by. I pretended I could see and thanked him politely. Then I quickly asked him to tell us about the schooner.

The story of the schooner was one we had heard many times but we liked to hear Mr. Elsworth tell it. It was always hard to believe.

"Just where did they build the schooner?" I asked (though I really knew).

"Right over thar by the side o' this ledge," Mr. Elsworth said. "A long time before my folks built our house, Josiah Swett built a cabin nigh here and he moved up with his family a good hundred years ago."

"Why did he come to live way up on a mountain?" Susan asked.

"I find a mountain a right good place to live," Mr. Elsworth said, "and anyhow there was a lot of big white-and-red oak and some beech trees just standing here when Josiah Swett decided to build himself a schooner. It was the kind of wood sailors liked to use to build sturdy ships. It was a two-masted schooner that he and his son, William, built together. They built it on a scoot or cradle."

We knew the best part of the story was to come. How, I always wondered, was the big boat brought down the mountain to the ocean?

"I reckon Josiah Swett had a powerful lot of friends," Mr. Elsworth said. "At any rate he got them to help him. After there was a snowfall and the roadbed was good, he got the farmers from all the towns around to come with their oxen. There were fifty yoke of oxen used. It was like a barn raising, hard work, but a good time for all. I guess the men decided if Swett had spent a year building the schooner they could help out for a few days. It was three days from the top of the mountain to Kennebunkport. The first night they stopped at Shaker Pond. They carried along food for the oxen and food and a barrel of rum for the men. They must have cleared everyone off the road ahead of them. It was some trick to keep all those oxen in line."

Mother asked if the schooner turned out to be a good seaworthy ship.

"Oh yes," Mr. Elsworth continued. "Young William Swett was the captain. He was just twenty years old and he made a heap of trips coastwise and to the West Indies. There's a record somewhere of a letter young William wrote to his father telling of a cargo of potatoes he carried from Mount Desert to Boston."

Mr. Elsworth walked along with us as we started slowly up the path to the summit. "You know," he said, "that schooner was named *Waterboro*. I guess everyone around here must have been mighty proud of it."

He talked as he walked, never losing his breath on the steep places and taking long, easy strides, one step for every three or four of mine or Susan's. In the field above his house, he pointed out the best places for picking blueberries and then he turned back.

The path was nearly hidden by the low blueberry bushes that covered the open ground almost to the top of the mountain. The berries were thickest close to big rocks or under low trees. They didn't always show plainly, but when I lifted up a branch I could see the choice big berries underneath. But now we could begin to see that strange, foreign land on the other side of our mountain and, though my legs were a little tired, I scrambled ahead to be the first to climb up on the granite summit. I don't know why I suddenly felt such a strong urge to reach the top quickly and to look out over the miles of country spread below. Of course I had a feeling of triumph in having walked so far, but much more than that, the unknown, which some day I would explore, was here and I hugged it to me with wonder and delight.

The day was perfect. The success of our walk always depended on seeing Mount Washington. Nothing else was as important, and on this day Mount Washington stood out clearly in the west, its pointed summit reaching far higher than the other mountains we could see. Was it possible that any mountain, anywhere, was higher?

The hills nearby were green, covered with forests of pine and oak but the distant White Mountains in New Hampshire were blue, blending softly with the sky. There was not a house in sight, though we knew there were many farms on the roads between the hills. There were three ponds but none as large as our lake, and now we turned from side to side looking at our familiar village and lake and then into the strange, exciting distance. We watched the shadow of a white cloud moving over the nearer hills, changing the woods to many different shades of green, and in one valley, making a little lake look deep purple. We saw a big bird circling below us and thought it might be a hawk. Several small swallows with scarcely a movement of their wings soared far out over the deep valley. How unafraid they were of the height! The stillness seemed to press in from every side and I pushed it off with my arms stretched over my head. How strong I felt! Susan and I tried shouting but the echo was very faint. The sun was warm and kind and the little breeze was fragrant.

On the way back to Howard Elsworth's house we filled our baskets very quickly with the plump blueberries. He was standing in his doorway as we came by and touched his battered gray hat as we called, "Thank you for the blueberries." His telescope was in his hand.

"When you get down to the store," he called, "tell Marsh there's a lot of smoke over by Parsonsfield; maybe a forest fire."

We always went down the mountain by a shorter route, one which was far too steep for the climb up. A half mile down we came to a group of sugar maples, and in the middle of them was Mr. Emery's maple sugar shack. We wished so much that we didn't have to be in school in Saco when the sap was running in the maple trees and the sugaring off was taking place over a big log fire. Mr. Emery had told us how good it tasted when the hot syrup was poured on the snow to harden.

The only other landmark that we welcomed with special interest on the way down was a brook with sandy banks where blue fringed gentian grew. We picked just a few, full of awe at their rare blue color, and wondered about the sandy banks because once some grains of gold had been panned there by Mr. Emery.

When we reached the house we were hot and dusty. How far behind us the cool top of the mountain seemed. Grandfather looked at our baskets of berries but didn't think much of the quantity we had brought back. He could see no reason for our long walk except to get a large amount of blueberries.

I hurried into the kitchen and pumped a cold drink of water for each of us while Susan and Mother measured the blueberries into a tin quart measure and from that into a big, yellow kitchen bowl. We had nearly four quarts, quite enough for a pie and blueberry muffins and for blueberries on our breakfast cereal. Then we put our flowers in a blue ginger jug. Some were quite wilted but they all were precious because each one represented a happy spot where we had stopped.

The next thing was to give Marsh Howard Elsworth's message about the smoke in Parsonsfield. The only telephone in the village was at the store and Marsh could call the pleasant telephone girl in Bar Mills and she would tell everyone up the line to watch out for a possible fire. I ran down the road to the store and delivered the message, and when I got back we started for the lake and our swim. It had been a lovely day.

EIGHT

The Blacksmith

Onvil Sawyer, the blacksmith, was a friend of Grandfather's and of us children as well. His shop was a square, squat little building with a slanting roof that came down low over the eaves. It faced the country road that was the main street of the village, and its front door was as wide as a barn door so that a horse and wagon could drive inside. Both outside and inside were crusted with black soot from the smoke of the forge. I thought the shop looked like a big inkwell squashed down on the edge of a green field. It was a great contrast to the white farmhouses farther down the village road.

The big forge was on the back wall of the shop. It was a platform of brick about five feet square and raised several feet from the floor. A bed of coke smoldered slowly in it until the big, leather bellows beside the forge were pumped, and then it glowed red and yellow with little spurts of blue flame. An open chimney above the forge took most of the smoke away, but if I looked toward the light, I could see slender blue spirals of smoke floating up toward the black rafters. The heavy rough planks of the floor were black, and around the forge and by the workbenches they were covered by at least an inch of metal filings. Deeper piles, together with scraps of wood and iron, had been swept under the benches.

Hanging on wooden pegs near the forge were iron wagon rims of different widths and sizes and the blades of sickles and scythes. Along one of the side walls there was a long workbench with several iron vises for holding pieces of wood or metal that were being worked on. The racks of tools were above the bench, and there were a dozen or more hammers, some of them small, others great sledgehammers. There were gimlets and chisels and a wonderful row of shining draw shaves. There were also three or four kegs of nails. These seemed like great wealth to me because Grandfather had only two coffee cans half full of nails on his shelf in the barn.

On Saturday evenings, with his face and hands shining from a hard scrubbing, Mr. Sawyer would come to our house to eat beans and brown bread with us, and to play a game or two of pitch with Grandfather. He ate beans by balancing them on his knife and quickly transferring them to his mouth. He had a neatly trimmed black beard, but his mustache was long, and the ends drooped so low that he drank his tea by sucking it in so as not to get the ends inside the cup. Susan and I watched him intently, and sometimes Mother had to shake her head at us. He was a quiet man, and I thought he seemed sad. He talked very little at the table except to say "Yes Ma'm" or "No Ma'm" to Mother. But after supper he would talk with Grandfather about the new road that was being built around the mountain or the high price of wagon rims.

I liked to walk through the field behind the blacksmith shop and look in at the back door. Mr. Sawyer owned the field and the grass was thin and coarse and never cut, so it was full of daisies and buttercups and devil's paintbrush. Often, I would step quietly inside the shop and watch Mr. Sawyer work. He was a tall man with strong arms and hands. He worked with the sleeves of his gray cotton shirt rolled up. His trousers hung loosely from suspenders and were made of some sort of black cloth that didn't show dirt very much. His left shoulder was hunched up higher than the right because for years he had used his left arm to pump the heavy bellows. With his right hand he always held the tongs which gripped a piece of metal that was being heated red hot in the coals.

When he was going to shoe a horse, he would first lift up its hoof and pare it smooth, slowly and deliberately while the horse got used to him. Then, putting the hoof down, he heated the shoe until it was white hot. He worked very quickly at this point, pumping the bellows as fast as he could, and the minute the shoe was ready he transferred it to the anvil, and with firm, strong strokes of his hammer, he pounded it into the right shape. Next, he would plunge the shoe for an instant into the tub of water that stood nearby, seize the horse's foot and, holding the hoof tightly against his leather apron, swiftly hammer the shoe on. There would be a strange, strong smell when the still warm metal touched the hoof, but Mr. Sawyer talked soothingly to the horse all the time, and it was usually quiet. I shivered to think what would happen if the horse should suddenly kick, and I stood way back by the door.

I especially liked to watch Mr. Sawyer shape the rim of a wagon wheel. The hot metal would gleam red and yellow on the forge, and when he transferred it to the anvil and hammered it, first with heavy blows, and then accurate exact taps, the sparks scattered and flew high up to the black rafters. I liked, too, to see the clouds of white steam rise when the hot metal was plunged into the tub of water by the forge. This, I understood, was to set the shape.

One day I was watching the shower of golden sparks when two big ones fell on my cotton dress. I wasn't sure that Mr. Sawyer even knew I was there, but in a second he doused me with water. I had no idea he could move so fast. It was the only time he ever sounded cross. "Stand back, child," he said.

When Mr. Sawyer was not too busy, he would let me use some of the tools by the long bench to make shingle boats. I clamped a shingle in the vise and, carefully holding the two wooden handles of the draw shave, pulled it toward me along the shingle. Smooth thin curls of wood fell on the floor as I made a point at one end, and if the wood was clean and light, I liked to put the shavings in my hair and pretend I had blonde curls instead of heavy brown braids. After I had rounded the back of my boat, I took the shingle out of the vise and, with a gimlet, made a hole in the center for a mast, which was usually a thin sliver from another shingle. Then Mr. Sawyer wedged a little piece of wood in the back for the rudder. This was hard to do without splitting the shingle. Then he would rummage under the bench for a piece of birch bark which I could tack to the mast for a sail. Together we tried out the boat in the tub of water by the forge to see if it balanced well and later I would take it down to the lake.

Mr. Sawyer seemed to enjoy having me make boats. Once he said, "My son John used to make shingle boats."

One day I found a bundle of new shingles in our barn. I knew Grandfather had bought them to patch a leak in the woodshed roof, but I thought I could pull two or three out of the bottom of the pile without his missing them. I made two beautiful clean boats, and it was so much fun that I took half a dozen more shingles and went back to the blacksmith shop. Mr. Sawyer looked at me questioningly. "Guess your Grandpa needs those," he said. I felt suddenly ashamed and quickly ran back to our barn to return the shingles.

Mr. Sawyer's home was like a box perched on the rafters in a corner of the shop. It wasn't more than ten feet square. To reach it, he had to climb up a ladder nailed to one wall of his shop, push up a trapdoor, and pull himself into the little room.

On the rare times I was invited to climb up, it seemed very scary to pull myself over the edge, but when the trapdoor was closed and the small braided rug spread down, I was in a quite different place from the smoky shop below. The walls were rough boards, but they had been painted white. The room was over less than half of the shop, and on one side was a window that looked down on the long workbench and toward the forge. Mr. Sawyer could look out of this window and see anyone who came in the big door. On the other side a great wide window looked out on the meadow, and in the afternoon the western sun streamed in.

There was a narrow cot in this room, covered with a blue-and-white patchwork quilt spread neatly over the bedclothes. Under the cot was a storage trunk. On one wall were some hooks for Mr. Sawyer's clothes, and over them hung a blue denim curtain. There was a small sink on one wall, but Mr. Sawyer had to carry the water up from the pump below. Above the sink was a small closet with a few dishes and shelves for storing groceries, and below the sink hung a frying pan and two or three kettles. Mr. Sawyer cooked on a two-burner kerosene stove which he carefully placed in the sink before lighting so that there would be no danger of fire.

A small round table with a marble top stood under the big window, and on it was a kerosene lamp, a big Bible with a red plush cover, and a picture of Mr. Sawyer's wife who had died some years before. There was also a picture of his youngest son taken when he was eighteen. Grandfather told me the son was now a grown-up man and lived in Texas. Grandfather thought Mr. Sawyer had quarreled with his son and didn't want to hear from him. I was sure Grandfather was wrong, especially after noticing how anxiously Mr. Sawyer waited for the mail every day.

Mr. Sawyer was always among the group of men who waited for the stage on Marsh Cousens' front porch. One day

I noticed him restlessly walking into the store and out again. On the counter in the store was a long slab of hard chewing tobacco, and a cutter for measuring it. Mr. Sawyer cut himself off a plug and paid for it, but he put it in his pocket without chewing any. Mr. Newcomb, who always waited for the stage too, asked him, just to pass the time of day, if he expected some mail. Mr. Sawyer said he reckoned he would get a letter from Texas.

When Len drove up and delivered the mail pouch, Marsh took it behind the glass barricade of mailboxes. He always took his time sorting the mail. This was his one important hour when everyone had to wait for him. Len walked over to the big wheel of store cheese and sliced off a thin piece with his jackknife. Then he picked up a round common cracker from the barrel by the counter and slapped the two together. He ate this half leaning against the counter as he waited to take the mail pouch on to Limerick.

I had been sent to get our mail and, by peeking through one of the boxes, I could see Marsh studying each letter carefully as if passing judgment on it before placing it in its proper box. Then he leaned out over the counter and called to Mr. Sawyer. "Here, Onvil, I guess you got the address wrong on this one. It's come back." He handed him the letter in such a way that everyone could see that the address was crossed out and UNKNOWN was written in big black letters across the envelope. Mr. Sawyer took it without saying a word and abruptly walked out.

It was not long after this when the gypsies came to Waterboro. They came almost every year and camped in the woods below our field, but we never knew when it would happen until one morning we looked out of the window and there were their tents and wagons. It was a small gypsy band— not over three tents and three or four wagons. The unpainted, high-sided wagons were pulled by two horses each, and they were piled full of tents and clothes and kitchen utensils, and what looked like rags. Women and children rode in the middle of the wagons, and the men crowded onto the drivers' seats or walked beside the thin horses. Shortly after they were settled, one of the men would come to the door and say to Grandfather, "We are here. Is it all right with you?"

Grandfather never told them to leave although he grumbled about the danger of a grass fire. He was just a little afraid to send them away. I was never allowed to walk alone down to the camp. Gypsies were said to steal things and kidnap children.

One morning, right after the gypsies had arrived, Mr. Sawyer came by our house as I was standing by the gate. "Ask your mother if you can go a piece down the road with me to see the gypsies," he said. I ran into the house, half expecting that mother would say no, but she said I could go and gave me twenty-five cents to buy a berry basket.

The gypsy camp seemed full of hungry dogs that sniffed at our heels, and there were three or four boys and girls playing tag around and under the wagons. One tent near the road had a poster in front of it with a big, red hand and the word FORTUNES painted on it. In front of another tent, two women were sitting on the grass making baskets. They were using long pieces of raffia which were soaking in a pail of water. I had never seen women with such black hair and such brown faces. When they smiled, their teeth looked very white. They wore long brass earrings, and many chains of beads around their necks. Their full, long skirts were bright red and orange. As I stopped to look, one of them gave me a friendly smile and patted the grass beside her, asking me to sit down. At first, I felt a little frightened, but it was fun to watch her swift fingers making a basket.

"Stay here and watch," Mr. Sawyer said. "I'll be right back," and before I could say anything he went into the Fortune tent.

In a few minutes he was back and as he stood by the entrance to the tent I could hear his last words to the fortune teller. "So you think he is all right, do you? But you can't tell when . . . ?"

There was a murmur in the tent, and Mr. Sawyer seemed to be listening carefully. Then, we walked back slowly toward our house. I had my new berry basket, and I stopped every few feet to pick the low bush blueberries that grew in patches by the road. Mr. Sawyer seemed to be thinking. He stopped beside me as I picked, but sometimes he would not walk along until I had moved some way ahead of him. I wished with all my heart he would not be so quiet. I wished he would tell me about his son.

When we reached our gate he patted my shoulder. "Come on down to the shop after dinner," he said. "I've got a real good piece of wood you can have to make a boat."

NINE

Maine Winter

We had come to Waterboro only once in the winter, but I often wished Mother would take us up there again when all the fields were white and the lake was covered with ice. I sometimes thought about that snowy trip as I rowed on the lake on a hot summer day and I wondered if Grandfather and his brothers and sisters had skated on the lake and if they had gone sliding on the long hills.

Winters in Maine were long and severe. Snow usually fell in early November, and the ground was not bare again until late March. Susan and I were glad when the hard, brown earth was covered with snow and we could bring our sleds down from the barn chamber.

The street in front of Grandfather's house in Saco was long and straight, and in winter it was a favorite place for sleigh races. To make the road passable after a storm a big wooden roller was dragged along over the snow by two horses. Then, as sleighs and pungs and sledges drove by, they flattened the snow down even more until it became a smooth road. When some spots were worn bare, or the ruts got deep, the men shoveled the snow from the sides back into the street so that it was smooth again for the runners of their sleighs.

The sidewalk was cleared by Tim Cassidy, an Irishman, with a wooden plow which was just the width of the sidewalk. It was pulled by his big gray workhorse that was blind in one eye. After a snow fall we could hear Tim coming down the street, shouting to his horse to keep him in the middle of the sidewalk. To make the plow more effective, Tim stood on it, and he kept his balance in a remarkable way as the plow moved slowly over the uneven walk. We used to stand by our gate to watch him go by.

We always dug out our own walk from the gate to the front door, and beyond that to the kitchen door. Grandfather shoveled smoothly without lifting too much at a time, but Susan and I loved to cut big cubes of the snow and, using all our strength, toss them first on one side and then on the other until the path had walls of snow as high as our waists. When the air was crisp and the sun sparkling on clean, white drifts, this was an exhilarating chore. Sometimes when the snow was very deep and unmarked, we lined up with a friend or two, and all of us fell over backward together and rubbed our arms back and forth to make "angel wings" beside the imprint of our bodies in the snow. Then we took sticks and printed names for our angels.

If the snow was sticky, that was the time to make a snowman. Starting with a small snowball, I would roll it around the yard, picking up more and more snow with each revolution. Finally, it was so big and heavy that I couldn't move it a bit farther, even when I put my shoulder against it and pushed with all my might; and that was where the snowman had to stand. A smaller ball went on top of the big one for his head, an old broom was stuck beside him and coal from the cellar made his eyes. Grandfather let me take one of his old hats as a final touch.

When soft clean snow had just fallen on the kitchen windowsill, Mother would let me open the window quickly and fill a bowl with snow. Then I sprinkled it with sugar and the juice of an orange. It made snow ice cream which had to be eaten fast before it melted.

A little way from our house was a street that sloped down to the river. Children came from all around to slide there. Sleighs had to use the street too, because it led to Biddeford; but somehow children on sleds and people in sleighs managed to look out for one another. If I saw a sleigh catching up with me, I knew it was wise to roll off in a snowdrift on the side.

The children who were most expert in sliding went downhill "belly bump." I thought it was fun to drag one foot at the bottom of the hill. This took me around a sharp corner and, without stopping, down another hill. But the best winter sport of all was catching rides on pungs. Our grocer had a long, low pung in which he delivered orders. There was plenty of room in the back for three children to sit and hang their feet over the tailboard. He always slowed down for us to get on. As I got a little braver, I found I could keep my balance and stand on the runners of a pung and hold on to the side. The next step was to jump off while the sleigh was moving and catch a pung in another direction. How kind most drivers were! Children were on all the pungs in town with the exception of a few whose drivers swung their long whips and shouted for everyone to keep away. Of course, daring boys tried especially hard to meet this challenge and get on the forbidden pungs.

In early September, when Grandfather drove us back to Saco, because it was time for school, we said goodbye to the places we loved all summer, and we didn't expect to see them again before the following June. But one winter the unexpected happened. Mr. and Mrs. MacIntire lived three houses from us on North Street in Saco. Mr. MacIntire's mother, who was quite elderly, lived in Waterboro Center, and insisted on staying there alone through the winter in spite of her son's urgent invitation to come to Saco. Mr. MacIntire worried about her.

One shiny February day, he stopped by the house to say he had heard "the going" was good, and he planned to drive to Waterboro Center for Washington's Birthday. Would we like to go too?

Mother had a Sunday school class of high school boys.

Five of them had had perfect attendance for a year, and Mother wanted to give them a special treat. This was the opportunity she had been wishing for. If Mr. MacIntire would let the five boys and Susan and me ride to Waterboro in his pung, she would go ahead by trolley and train and get the house open and warm. One of the five boys was Mr. MacIntire's son, so that made his decision easy. It was a little harder to persuade Grandfather that we would do no harm either to ourselves or the house.

To reach Waterboro by train, Mother had to take a trolley at six in the morning. It ran fifteen miles to Portland, and there she could get a train on the back division of the Boston & Maine for East Waterboro, then Len Doughty would take her the two miles to Waterboro Center. She would arrive by ten in the morning, and the sleigh ride would bring us there several hours later.

It was dark as night when she woke me and whispered that she was leaving, and that oatmeal for breakfast was cooking on the back of the kitchen stove. I watched her as she walked down the street to catch the trolley. I could just see her by the light of the gas lamp on the corner. She was carrying a basket with two jars of clams in it which she had prepared for a chowder to be eaten on our arrival in Waterboro. Grandfather was stirring in his room and I guess he, too, was watching Mother. I didn't think then what a long, cold trip she was taking.

Our ride was pure delight. The February sun was high. The whole world was white and silver. The bottom of Mr. MacIntire's pung was filled with straw; bags and boxes were pushed under the driver's seat and sleds were hooked on behind. We all sat in the straw with our backs against the sides of the pung and our feet in front of us. We had blankets and robes over us but even so Susan and I were glad to be wearing the warm stocking caps and mittens Mother had knitted for us. The boys were Jimmy MacIntire, who was able to help his father with the horses, John Winslow who lived next door to us, Robert Duncan whose father was our doctor, and the Johnson twins. They were all wrapped up as warmly as we were.

The snow was packed down so hard that the runners squeaked as the pung slid along. The bells on the two horses sounded sharp and clear. The sky was the pale blue of winter and seemed to merge with the piled-up drifts. In the fields there was a soft layer of snow on top of crust. Sometimes the wind blew the loose snow in curling patterns, and sometimes picked it up and whirled it like fine powder into our faces which soon became crimson from the cold.

All the familiar landmarks, which we loved to meet in the summer, were changed by the snow. The fields looked bigger, the woods darker and denser. Some of the birch trees were bent over so that their tops were imprisoned in the snow, but the pines were straight and tall, and held up immense burdens which sometimes fell off with a sudden dull boom. In spots where the trees were coated with ice, the sun made them sparkle so that we could scarcely keep our eyes open.

For a while everyone sat quietly in his place as the horses jogged along evenly on the level road; but this couldn't last.

It was easy to lean out and reach a handful of snow, and before long snowballs were flying at the fence posts. Pretty soon the boys were jumping out and standing on the runners or wrestling with one another in the snow. Mr. MacIntire didn't look around, but drove steadily on. Only once, when two boys got too far behind and called in distress, did he pull the horses up and say that everyone must stay in the pung. They were bringing in so much snow on their feet that we all were cold.

When we crossed the river, the water looked black through the ice and the pung slewed on the crusted planks of the bridge. Once Jimmy MacIntire yelled for us to look over by some bushes, and we saw a red fox standing near a log. He was not scared, but put his tawny tail out and walked slowly into the woods. Once we passed a low sledge piled high with pine logs. It was being pulled by a yoke of oxen whose breath made white clouds around their heads. The oxen plodded along with an even, powerful gait.

As we got near Waterboro we could see our mountain. It seemed cold and distant. Grandfather's house looked naked with all the leaves off the maple trees. We drove up just as Peleg Gooch was finishing a path to the front door with a big wooden shovel. Mother must have waded in.

Fires were burning in the living-room and dining-room fireplaces, and even in the Franklin stove in the parlor. The big, black kitchen stove was giving off the most heat, and clouds of steam were coming from the teakettle. There was a delicious smell of clam chowder. Mr. MacIntire came in to make sure the pump in the kitchen sink was working, and

Mother told him Peleg had gone down cellar and attached it for her. She was busy making hot biscuits to go with the chowder.

We were to stay two nights with one whole day sandwiched between our sleigh rides up and back from Saco to Waterboro. The lumbermen, logging on the mountain, had pounded the snow down so that we could slide for a mile or more if we wished to walk up that far. The ice on the lake was thick and smooth for skating. Far out from the shore were five or six smelt houses in which fishermen could sit and keep warm while fishing through holes in the ice. Jimmy MacIntire brought along three lures for catching fish. He cut holes and put down lines baited with salt pork and fixed red flags on sticks so that they would snap up if a fish bit. We stood hopefully around the holes, waiting for bites, but we had to stamp our feet to keep warm, and maybe we scared the fish away. In the end, Jimmy caught two pickerel and Mother cooked them for his breakfast.

How Mother fed us we didn't know. The cold, crisp air made us very hungry. She got Mrs. Tompkins to come up to help her make countless pancakes and fried eggs, beef stew and cornbeef hash. The boys' mothers had sent cakes and cookies with them, but they soon disappeared.

There was no heat upstairs in the house, and Grandfather had worried about this, but Mother had a plan. In the evening she asked the boys to bring all the feather beds and pillows downstairs to warm them around the kitchen stove. Then, while we popped corn in front of the dining-room fire, she heated soapstones to put in the beds. The only very cold spot was the privy which had to be reached by a dash through the woodshed into the barn.

When I had made the final run up the stairs and had put on my flannel nightgown and jumped into bed, I could feel the cold pressing around my head. I settled down deep into my warm feather bed and pulled the blankets up to my ears. I woke in the night for just a few minutes as the icy branches of the maple outside my window rattled and tapped, and I realized I was toasty warm. The back stairs gave a familiar creak, and I heard a thump, thump in the next bedroom as someone kicked out a soapstone that was no longer needed.

In the morning the village street looked very bare to me though smoke was coming out of the neighbors' chimneys. It was thin and rose straight up in the air. Many of the houses were banked with branches of fir and pine to keep out the cold, and the cows and chickens were in the big barns. The only busy spot I could find was Mr. Sawyer's blacksmith shop where he was straightening some iron runners that were to be nailed on a sleigh. In the store Mr. Elsworth was sitting on a nail keg beside the round iron stove. Every little while he would spit tobacco juice on the top of the stove, and it would bounce around in a little ball and disappear. He told me he had been in Widow Hobbs' house after the last blizzard, and her room was as "cold as an orchard in the winter with the bars let down." Later, we often quoted this saying.

Near our boathouse were two fallen trees. The boys pulled them to the edge of the ice, and with pine cones and a stump of pitch pine they made an enormous bonfire. All of them were very good skaters, and the Johnson twins skated all the way across the lake. I liked to get on my sled at the top of the bank, and see how far I could skim out over the ice. It was scary to think of it as the deep, deep water we had rowed over during the summer.

The days in winter are short. Before we knew it the sun was sinking, and the shadows on the snow were turning purple. We waited until we could see the first star between the branches of the pines, and then we piled snow on the fire and walked back to the house.

On the return trip the next morning, Mother rode on the seat with Mr. MacIntire. Just before we left she baked some potatoes which were piping hot. We stuffed them in our pockets to keep our hands warm, and it was surprising to see how long they kept their heat. We were all glad to cover up snugly with the extra blankets Mother had taken from the house, for the wind was cold.

Mother had a soft, sweet soprano voice, but she found it hard to sing on key. She knew, however, that Mr. MacIntire sang in the church choir so, with her urging, he started us all singing "John Brown's Body" and "Annie Laurie" and "Jingle Bells," and many others. There was much joking— and boasting too—about who could skate the fastest or eat the most biscuits. I looked out over the side of the pung at the cold white world, and thought the next time I traveled on this road, the world would be warm and green again.

TEN

The Newcombs

During the winter in Saco, Mother went calling about once a week. She wore her Sunday clothes and carried a little card case that held her calling cards. She always followed a strict rule about leaving cards in a silver plate on the hall stand of each friend she visited, even though she knew the person very well. Once in a while she asked me to go with her but I didn't like it very much. It was hard to sit quietly in a slippery parlor chair and listen to grown-up conversation, although I felt better about it when I was given a generous slice of tea cake.

In Waterboro Center we went to see people but we didn't make formal calls except for the two occasions when we called on the Newcomb sisters. Miss Elvira and Miss Eleanor Newcomb were spinsters who lived a half mile outside our village on Durgin's Ridge. Their father ran a ten-acre farm there and the two sisters helped him as much as they could. All three lived in a white saltbox house, so surrounded by apple trees that only a little part of the roof showed from the road. A narrow, winding path led uphill through a meadow to their gate.

On two Sundays during the year, usually in July when we had just come to Waterboro Center, and again in September before we left for Saco, Mother, Susan and I made a call on the Newcombs. We went on Sundays so that we could wear our best clothes. We knew the sharp eyes of the Newcomb sisters would be looking at every detail and that they would not consider it a proper compliment to them unless we were dressed up. They could sew very well, Mother knew, and it was very likely that they would copy whatever dress she wore during the long winter months when they were snowbound.

On one of these Sundays in July, we started to walk up the hill in the early afternoon. Mother wore a soft, white muslin dress. The waist had a high-boned collar trimmed on the top with Irish crochet lace. Susan and I wore our white cotton sailor suits. The broad blue collars had three rows of braid around the edges and we had black taffeta hair ribbons on the ends of our braids. We were wearing our best boots and we tried not to scratch them by kicking our toes against the rocks in the road. We walked slowly, going up the path through the meadow. Two cows at the edge of the road lifted their heads to look at us but they didn't move toward us. We were glad of this for Susan was a little afraid of cows. Halfway up the hill was a single apple tree that shaded a spring crowded with mossy rocks which almost concealed the water. Two baby frogs plopped in as I pushed some long grass away; when a little green garter snake slithered under a rock I decided to postpone having a drink. But we stopped to look at the view of our lake. We could see a part of Black Cove surrounded by its hemlocks and across the water, through a break in the trees, were the Limington hills.

The gate in the white picket fence in front of the New-comb house was stiff from disuse and creaked as Mother opened it. It was evident that the kitchen door at the other end of the house was used more often, but we walked po-litely toward the front door. The granite flagstones that led from the gate had been there so long that they were sunk deep in the grass and were covered with lichen and patches of green moss.

On one side of the walk was an old dory, painted white and filled with purple-and-white petunias. (I wished Mother would plant petunias in Uncle Lon's green dory that was lying behind our barn. It was too leaky to use in the lake any more.) On the other side of the walk was a bed of pink phlox and of tall, fragrant mignonette. The front door was painted green and the narrow sidelights on either side of it were filled with bluish, opaque bull's-eye glass that Miss Elvira often told us had been put in by her grandfather.

Mother pulled the purple glass knob beside the door and we could hear a faint, silvery bell ringing inside the house.

It was not answered for several minutes and we realized we had walked up the hill too fast, for when the door was opened and the sisters appeared it was apparent that their black alpaca dresses had just been hooked up. Miss Elvira's cameo pin was crooked and Miss Eleanor's face was flushed and some strands of gray hair had straggled down from the neat bun on top of her head. Miss Elvira and Miss Eleanor had worked hard all their lives, as women on farms must do. They churned their own butter, took care of the hens, did the housework and washing and helped with the vegetable garden. Sometimes they were seen in the hayfield, both wearing Shaker sunbonnets to keep the sun from their faces.

In spite of her hard work, Miss Eleanor had a delicate complexion. She had a narrow, aristocratic nose and thin lips which she moved very little in speaking. Miss Elvira looked much like her but she was a little stooped and had a restless habit of biting her lips like a rabbit eating lettuce, and she looked at us shyly as if hoping for approval. They were quiet women, with gentle voices, and a great desire to be thought of as ladies and as more genteel than their neighbors. Grandfather once said that their airs didn't set well with their neighbors but Mother thought they must be lonely.

To make up for not being sociable, they spent many hours making beautiful drawn-in rugs. Their living room showed that they wished to be different. It was a room with a low ceiling and deep-set windows with heavy wooden shutters. (I wondered if these shutters had been put in long ago when Indians were still roaming around.) In the middle of the room was a square oak table and in the exact center of the table stood a large kerosene lamp. Its china base was painted with yellow roses and the shade was of yellow glass. The sisters' neat workbaskets were on either side of the table and perhaps three outdated copies of the *Atlantic Monthly* lay in a precise pile near the lamp. These, I remembered, had been given to them by Mother at least two years ago.

On the mantel above the fireplace was a row of pewter plates and above these hung a Revolutionary flintlock musket. In front of the fireplace was a dark blue, hooked rug; its pattern was a strange-looking white dog lying in the middle of a bunch of red roses. In front of the pine grandfather's clock was a round rug with a green border and purple flowers in the center. Another rug was in stripes of green, red and black. They were all made from wool clothes the sisters had worn and a few pieces had come from Mother. The designs had been made by Miss Elvira.

Another occupation on which the sisters spent many hours was tracing their family tree back as far as possible. They were direct descendants of one of the Wentworths who had been a governor of New Hampshire in Colonial times, and a picture of him, dressed in knee britches with a powdered wig and a great, gold chain around his neck, hung on one wall of the living room. Under it, in a wide gold frame, was Miss Eleanor's certificate of membership in the Daughters of the American Revolution. The sisters had discovered that we, too, could trace a relationship to the Wentworths and so they felt they were related to us. Their conversation was full of references to this remarkable fact and Mother, at one time, had been given a picture of Lady Wentworth dressed in court robes and wearing a tiara. We children were delighted when Miss Elvira said Mother looked like her. On the wall opposite the picture of Governor Wentworth was a steel engraving of the trial of the Earl of Strafford. He, too, was a very real person to the Newcomb sisters who thought of him as a near relative.

I spent much of my time during our call looking at this picture. I really wanted to go out in the yard but I knew I must be polite and sit still. My dress was too hot for a warm summer day and my long white cotton stockings made my legs itch. The picture of the Earl showed him before his accusers in the House of Commons. I only half listened to Mother and the Newcomb sisters. Instead I tried to count the number of heads in the picture.

At length Miss Elvira excused herself and went to the kitchen to make tea. At the same time Mr. Newcomb came to the living room doorway and beckoned to me. Susan and I looked at Mother who nodded assent and we hurried into the kitchen where glasses of milk and fat molasses cookies were waiting for us. Since we had been sitting still so long listening to grown-up conversation, we were very hungry.

Mr. Newcomb was a heavyset man with a red face and big hands that were rough and swollen. There was a faint, pleasant smell of cows and hayfields about him. He never came into the living room while his daughters were entertaining callers, but we children liked his quiet laugh and had been hoping all afternoon that he would invite us out to see his stuffed birds.

He led us now into a back room where there was a long table covered with old newspapers, neatly spread out, and on it were crowded several hundred birds which he had mounted. (At the time it did not occur to us to wonder if he had shot the birds.) We were excited to hunt out the ones we knew and were happy to recognize a thrush and a bluebird and a chickadee. At one end of the table was a loon. We had never seen a loon near to and looked with wonder at its long, sleek body and the black neck with its white collar. The loons lived at the end of our lake and we often tried to get near them in our rowboat but they were so smart in ducking beneath the water that we had never caught up with them.

Mr. Newcomb plainly enjoyed pointing out the unusual birds to us, especially a little hummingbird which he had mounted on a petal of a cardboard lily. He was as proud of his hobby as his daughters were of their rugs and their ancestors. Mr. Newcomb had once kept his collection in the living room but when it grew too large his daughters made him move it into the back room.

I could dimly remember calling on the Newcombs long ago with my father. It was during a vacation our family had spent with Grandfather in that faraway time when my father was living. I was a very small girl and Father would let me sit in a little wire seat strapped to the handle bars of his bicycle. We often went to see sick people, and Miss Elvira Newcomb was ill in the hospital so Father rode up to see her sister and father. After a while, I remember, we all knelt down by our chairs and Father said a prayer but, though

I put my hands over my face, I peeked all the time at the birds and didn't hear a word of the prayer. The loon's shiny eyes seemed to be looking at me. I thought of this again as I put my hand gently on the loon's back.

But now it was time to go home. Mother called us into the living room to say goodbye to Miss Eleanor and Miss Elvira. Mr. Newcomb had disappeared. His daughters' goodbye manners were too difficult for him.

The sisters did not want to let us leave. They walked out into the garden with us and Miss Eleanor picked a bouquet of phlox and the fragrant mignonette. Miss Elvira hurried back into the house and brought out a half pound of butter she had churned the day before. It was in two neat squares, stamped with a sheaf of wheat. She had wrapped it in a white cloth and put it in a berry box.

We walked slowly down the hill, although Susan and I felt like running and skipping. We knew the Newcomb sisters looked forward to our call, and we felt sure they were watching us from behind the shutters in their living room.

ELEVEN

A Strange Illness

I was usually a well little girl, except for the times when my love of candy led to a bilious attack or I caught cold in the winter, but once I was really ill and it was in the summer at Waterboro. It started after an especially happy day. I had rowed Mother up the lake to Loon Island in the hope of seeing the loons. The sky was slightly overcast and the air was cool and delicious. It made me feel like rowing hard. I remembered the time I had nearly bumped into a mother loon and her two fluffy babies, and I was sure I could out-smart them again. When we caught sight of a mother and father loon in the distance, I stuck the oars in deep and pulled until the boat seemed to skim along more swiftly than ever before, but the loons disappeared under the water and I could not guess where they would come up.

For nearly an hour, Mother and I played hide-and-seek with the loons but finally we gave up and decided to go back to the boathouse. I drew in the oars and for a moment we floated quietly with some little waves pushing us toward the shore. Then, suddenly, we heard a strange screech in the tall pines on the bank. It sounded like a person who was hurt and it scared me, but Mother said, "That must be an owl. Something has disturbed his daytime sleep."

One of the wonderful things about seeing the outdoor world with Mother was that she made me feel that the discovery of a new flower or a new bird was a very great adventure. It was like an explorer finding a new land. There was something magical about getting acquainted for the first time with a bird that had lived all along in the nearby woods but which I had never seen before.

I was excited to find the owl and I rowed quickly to the bank of the lake which, at this place, had no sandy shore. There were alderbushes and birch trees bending over the water and, behind them, the tall pines and thick hemlocks made the woods look dark. I scrambled up the steep bank and stepped a little timidly into the deep shade and then, right over my head, a great gray bird with big, wide wings flew away from the top of a pine. He bumped blindly into another pine, swerved away, and with a slow, strong beat of his wings, disappeared among the hemlocks. He hadn't made a sound. No wonder, I thought, he could pounce on a little bird in the night.

I wanted to follow him but Mother called that it was time to go home. The lake had been calm when we left the boathouse but now the wind was blowing heavily against us and an unexpected thunderstorm was coming down over the mountain. I wanted to row as quickly as possible across the middle of the lake, but the waves were high and Mother thought it was too dangerous. She said we must follow the shore and I knew she was right. The trees along the bank began to bend in the rising wind and I made very slow headway. My arms were beginning to ache. Mother tried to help by pushing forward on the oars as I pulled them back. Once, she suggested we might land and wait for the storm to pass. But I thought I could beat the rain—and I almost did.

We were coming around the point from Black Cove when we saw the gray curtain of rain sweeping toward us. It flattened out the waves and the drops of water seemed to bounce from the surface of the lake. In a minute it reached us. The cool rain felt very good to me at first. My hands were hot and I had two blisters, but by the time we reached the boathouse both Mother and I were wet and cold.

I was too tired to eat my supper that night and the next morning I was sick. I had never felt so strange before. It was like floating on my back in the lake, or as I imagined it would feel if I were lying on a big, fluffy summer cloud. The little gold oak leaves painted on the black footboard of my bed nodded and swayed as if they were dancing. I was not very uncomfortable nor even aware of being ill, but I was too tired to move and it seemed perfectly natural to be in bed looking at the strange things in my room. A big rose and a little rose in the pattern of the wallpaper became a lady with a frilly dress wheeling a small baby carriage, and I followed her with my eyes as she walked around the room.

Mother sat by my bed a lot of the time and put cold cloths on my head when it ached and tried to get me to eat. I thought her high black shoes looked like loons and I didn't like them to be so near.

Several days must have gone by. I don't remember much about them. Then, one day, I saw Dr. Duncan from Saco standing in the door. I thought I must be in Saco and that I had dreamed about Waterboro. Mother told me afterward that Grandfather had sent for Dr. Duncan and that he had driven all the way up to Waterboro Center in three hours and, after resting his horse, had gone right back.

Dr. Duncan was Scotch and, though he often seemed brusque, we liked him and thought he was very wise. He always wore a rumpled brown suit of some rough material and I sometimes imagined he looked like a shaggy St. Bernard. He had thick, sandy eyebrows and it seemed as though a long hair or two that straggled down from them might get into his eyes. He sat on the edge of my bed and asked me what I meant by chasing loons. When he drew those bushy eyebrows together and said, "Get well now," I thought it was an order. He carried a doctor's bag that had two sides which opened out flat and in it were rows and rows of small glass bottles filled with pills. When he opened the bag the pills jingled. He never came to our house without leaving an assortment. The bright pink ones, I knew, were for a stomach ache. Before pouring out the pills, he would hold the small bottle up with his thumb on the cork and shake it while the pills made a tiny muted sound. Then, without seeming to count, he would tip out an exact dozen or two onto a sheet from his prescription pad.

I was too sick to notice what he left after his visit to Waterboro, but when I got better I discovered three little heaps on a piece of white paper on the bureau. There were pink pills, pale green pills and white ones. Mother had covered them all with a clear drinking glass. I didn't know what they were supposed to be for, but I was very glad Dr. Duncan had not prescribed sulphur and molasses. This was the remedy he always prescribed in Saco in the early spring. Mother kept the jar of sulphur and molasses in the cold pantry and the molasses became so thick that it was hard to suck it off the spoon. But the good cold molasses hid the unpleasant taste of sulphur, and I thought warm sulphur and molasses would taste pretty bad in the summer.

Two days after Dr. Duncan's call I felt quite different. In a way it was not as pleasant. I had enjoyed the dancing flowers on my bed and sometimes I had floated away into a very delightful land. Now the bedroom looked just as it always had. I tried peeping quickly at the gold oak leaves but I could not catch them moving. Mother said I had been having "slow fever," the only name we ever had for this illness.

I got well rapidly, but after I was dressed and eating meals with the family I was still supposed to stay in the house for a week and lie down every afternoon. Up to this time Waterboro had been a place for outdoor fun, for swimming and rowing and picking blueberries, for climbing the mountain, for riding on hayloads, for walks in the woods. On rainy days I had explored the attic but Mother didn't want me to go up there while I still felt a little sick. I had been in bed for ten days and now the house looked very different to me, but when I forgot the disappointment of not going outside I was glad to have this quiet week of getting acquainted with it in a special way.

For the first time I really looked at the pictures. In every bedroom upstairs there were neatly framed mottoes embroidered in cross-stitch on stiff buckram. They said, "God is Love," "Love One Another," "Praise God." The prettiest one was in Mother's room. It showed an apple tree with red apples and a woman and man standing beside it. A second man with a raised axe stood next to the tree. The motto read, "Woodman, Spare That Tree."

The pictures on the walls downstairs had not been changed since Grandfather and his brothers and sisters were young. On one wall of the sitting room there was a large steel engraving of George Washington. He was standing by a table, Martha Washington was beside him sitting down, and he had his hand on her shoulder. In the picture their faces were smooth and unwrinkled as if they didn't have a thing to worry about. On the opposite wall in a very wide gold frame was a charcoal drawing called "The Old Mill." It had been drawn by Aunt Addie when she was a schoolgirl.

There were two pictures in the sitting room that had been sent home from California by Great-uncle Albert. One was an engraving of "Yohamite Falls" which Mother said was now "Yosemite" and the other was a picture of Uncle Albert's store. Uncle Albert had not been a gold miner but had run a store near the mines during the gold rush. It said on the picture that the store was in Columbia, California, but we couldn't find it in my geography so perhaps no one lived there any longer. Aunt Addie once told me he charged a dollar apiece for doughnuts.

I liked the blue plates in the dining room, which Mother had put on the mantel, and the colored prints of famous men on the walls. There was John Paul Jones holding a spyglass with his ship in the background. There was Henry Clay, sitting very straight on a strange horse that had an unnatural curve in its back and a very full tail that almost touched the ground, and there was Abraham Lincoln looking at a book with his little son, Tad.

But I liked best of all two small colored prints called "Little Sister" and "Little Brother." The little girl was wearing long white pantalettes below her blue dress and they reached down to her ankles. The little boy's coat was short in front with long tails behind. It was buttoned up to his chin and his wide black necktie was spread over it. The children had round faces and very neat hair. They looked as if they were always good. I imagined that Aunt Addie and maybe Grandfather had looked that way once.

I rarely went into the parlor. None of the chairs were comfortable because they were covered with black, slippery horsehair and they slanted forward so that it was hard not to slide off. But the parlor wallpaper was the prettiest in the

133

house. The pattern was of intertwining wreaths of many colored flowers. In one corner of the room was a walnut whatnot and on three shelves were luster china and little china figures. One small figure was a shepherd leaning against a tree and the tree trunk was a whistle. Once I put it to my lips and blew it softly. On the top shelf of the whatnot was a vase filled with peacock feathers.

Aunt Lu and Aunt Addie had made the frames for two pictures in the parlor. They had glued pine cones on a wooden background and painted the whole frame black. One picture was a pencil drawing by Aunt Lu called "A Castle on the Rhine."

It was fun to sit beside Mother on the sofa in the living room while she told me stories. My legs felt wobbly after being sick and I really didn't want to run outside. One day she pointed out some of the things that Grandmother and Aunt Addie and her sisters had made when they lived in the Waterboro house. (I thought they must have been awfully busy.) There were the patchwork quilts that were used on all our beds and two sofa pillows in the parlor with covers made of small triangles of silk and velvet joined together with cross-stitching. In the big chest, in the upstairs hall, were six pale yellow wool blankets that had been woven by hand with Great-grandmother's initials embroidered on them. I asked Grandfather if his father had kept sheep but he said the wool came from sheep raised by the Warrens in Limerick. The seven hand-woven linen sheets in this same chest were worn thin and felt smooth and slippery. They each had a seam down the middle where two widths of material were joined. Mother told me the small spinning wheel that Grandfather liked to keep in the dining-room window was for making linen thread, and the big one in the upper hall was for wool.

I had a chance to earn some money during the week I stayed in the house getting well. My allowance was ten cents a week and when I was outside Grandfather occasionally paid me ten cents for pulling weeds in his vegetable garden. Then, too, when the potato bugs came he paid me a penny for every five bugs I knocked off the plants into a can of kerosene. But it looked as if the potato bugs might be gone by the time I was well, so Mother offered to give me and Susan a cent for every ten flies we killed in the house.

The flies came in our kitchen door mostly and I'm afraid Susan and I did not try to keep them out. There was a small covered pail under the kitchen table in which we put the scraps from the table after each meal. Every noon Susan and I were supposed to carry the pail over to Mr. Stewart's and dump it in his pigpen. If we opened the kitchen screen door slowly a few extra flies came in. While I was sick, Susan had been going over alone and she was even slower than I about closing the door.

Another source of income was learning psalms. Mother renewed a standing offer of ten cents for every Psalm I learned by heart. The length of the psalm didn't matter, so at first I hunted up the shortest ones. I memorized the 117th which has only two verses and the 131st which has three verses, and I didn't think much about what they said. But after a while, as I turned the pages of my Bible, I found

I liked the 100th psalm so much that I wanted to learn it and I repeated it to myself in bed each night.

> "Make a joyful noise unto the Lord all ye lands.
> Serve the Lord with gladness; come before His
> presence with singing."

That was exactly the way I felt.

By the end of the week, I had earned fifty cents for psalms and eleven cents for flies.

TWELVE

Fourth of July

We were almost always in Waterboro on the Fourth of July. Susan and I sometimes thought regretfully of the Saco parade and of the band concert we would miss, but we tried to make up for it by buying firecrackers in Saco and taking them with us when we rode to Waterboro in Grandfather's surrey.

Next to the grocery store in Saco was Miss Selly's candy store and, during the month of June, she used one counter at the back of the store to display firecrackers. We could use our allowances and any small amounts we had earned for helping Mother or Grandfather to buy these, but it was very hard to get past the candy counter.

Miss Selley was short and had a big, misshapen lump on her back which made her hold her head back unnaturally. When she stood behind the counter, her head was not much above it. Her eyes darted quickly from one customer to another, and sometimes she spoke sharply, but she had great patience with us children, particularly when we were trying to decide on the best way to invest five cents in candy.

We liked to get penny candy that we could divide with each other, and with our friends. There were the long, black sticks of chewy licorice which could be pulled out to twice their length and then broken. There were white caramels, four for a cent, and peanuts with a sweet coating that made them look like baked beans. A minature bean pot full of these could be bought for a cent. In a glass jar on the shelf behind the counter were flat red candies about the shape and size of a nickel. These were five for a cent, and they had a sharp cinnamon taste and made my tongue red. In other jars were long twisted sticks of sugar candy in many flavors. Some were white with red lines of peppermint or green lines of lime, some were red with white lines of clove, and others clear yellow with a lemon flavor. These were a penny each and I could make mine last a long time by sucking the end slowly until it became a point and then gently licking the point until the whole delicious stick melted away.

As the time drew near for us to leave for Waterboro, we reluctantly walked past the candy counter because the firecrackers interested us more and more. Mother gave us each a dollar to add to our firecracker money, and we bought a variety of exciting packages. But it was just as difficult to choose the right firecrackers as it was to choose the right candy. There were Chinese firecrackers and torpedoes that were packed in boxes of sawdust so that they would not go off unexpectedly, and small boxes of caps which we stuck in a hole in the bottom of a special cane. They exploded with a satisfying bang when the cane was hit on the ground.

I usually chose the Chinese firecrackers because you got more for your money. The fuses of the small firecrackers were braided together into a close pack, and you could unwind them and set them off one by one to make them last. They cost five cents a package and I liked to get several of these rather than spending five cents apiece for cannon crackers— and anyway, we were not allowed to get giant cannon crackers because Grandfather said we might make a mistake and blow our fingers off.

In Waterboro Center anyone could tell that the Fourth of July was near at hand by watching Captain Jones who lived on the village square a short distance from our house. He was a wiry, erect man with a stiff, white mustache. He had a slight limp which he said came from a wound he got at the Battle of Gettysburg. He was very proud of this and of his rank in the army. He didn't farm his land like the rest of the people in the village, but he and his wife lived on his war pension.

He kept the small strip of grass in front of his place neatly trimmed, and near his front door was a carefully arranged pile of cannonballs. The cannonballs were surprisingly heavy, I thought. One time I tried to lift one and I could barely get if off the ground. It nearly fell back on my toes. The week before the Fourth of July, Captain Jones used to wipe the cannonballs and rub them with black stove polish. Then he replaced them in a pyramid.

He was in charge of the flagpole that stood in a triangle where three roads met, and he kept the big flag in his house. Each morning he would pull the flag to the top of the pole and then stand at attention for a moment. I tried to remember to run over and stand beside him.

Before Memorial Day the town clerk always bought new flags to be placed on the soldiers' graves in the cemetery behind the town hall, but it was Captain Jones who had a small, black notebook which held the names of everyone from our village who had fought in any war.

Just before the Fourth of July he inspected the cemetery flags to be sure they were standing up straight, and if any were torn he bought new ones to take their places. Then he would take his lawn mower to the cemetery and cut the grass on Jeremiah Tibbetts' grave, because there was no one left in the Tibbetts family to do this.

There were only two Revolutionary soldiers in our cemetery, Jeremiah Tibbetts and my great-great-grandfather, William Leavitt. Grandfather had not fought in the Civil War, but paid a $100 bounty for someone to take his place because he had to help his father in their big country store. His brothers, our Great-uncles Alonzo and James, had both been soldiers. Captain Jones sometimes reminded Grandfather of this, and he would suggest that Grandfather cut the grass on our lot long before it was really needed. Grandfather's face would get very red, and he would stamp up to the cemetery without saying a word.

The evening before the Fourth I always put my box of firecrackers on the hall table so they would be ready for the morning. It was fun to bang the torpedoes on the granite steps by the front door while every one in the house was asleep. It would have been easy to use up our firecrackers in the first two hours of the morning, but Susan and I tried to make our supply last as long as possible.

First, I would light a long stick of punk which gave off thin curls of smoke and glowed red when I blew on it. Punk was easier and safer to use than matches. Then I began by putting a firecracker or two by the road and lighting the short, white fuse which burned slowly when it was first touched with the punk, and then, about halfway to the fire-cracker, shriveled up in a fast rush which made me run to the steps until the expected explosion came.

As the morning went on, I got brave enough to hold a firecracker in my hand while lighting the fuse. For an ex-citing moment I held it, feeling this was enormously danger-ous, and then threw it in the air where it went off before touching the ground. I had discovered, too, that two or three crackers under a tin pail made an especially loud bang. We had bought some "snakes" at Miss Selly's store. These were small paper cones and when they were lighted a paper snake of astonishing length curled out of the cone. Mother came out on the steps to watch the snakes and marvel with us that they could come out of the little cones.

By noon we had only a few firecrackers left, and these we put aside to use the last thing before dark.

One Fourth of July the Sunday school of the Baptist Church was having a picnic at the lake. Suzy Abbot was a Baptist and she asked me to go swimming with her and the other children.

On the shore of the lake was a small crate, and in it was a very small pig. He was light brown with a black spot on his back and on one side. He was very clean, and his pink skin showed through his bristles. His little tail curled up and his moist flat nose was sniffing for something to eat. He wasn't much bigger than the tom cat at Marsh's store, and he looked at us out of his little, bright eyes, and gave short grunts of pleasure when we stuck pieces of pig weed into the crate.

Out from the bank of the lake a pole had been placed over the water and on the end of it was a red flag. The pole had been greased so that it was very slippery. The Baptist Sunday school superintendent announced that the little pig would be given to the boy or girl who could walk out on the pole and get the red flag. I wanted that little pig very much. I thought Grandfather could make a pen for it beside the barn, and I would feed my pig every day. The children lined up on the bank, and I was the eighth one. The pole was so slippery that it shone in the sun.

The first three boys took only two steps and went over into the water with a splash. Then came Mary Emery who took four steps, but at that point she felt sure of herself and stepped too quickly. With a shout and wild waving of her arms, she fell off. As I watched, I decided that those who had wet feet didn't have a chance. I stooped down and covered my feet with sand, and in a minute or two I was at the head of the line. I scuffed in the sand again, and started along the pole very slowly. When I took my sixth step, it was the farthest anyone had gone. I held my breath, but at this moment someone on the bank clapped his hands. I felt myself start and begin to slip. I took one more shaky step, and then made a desperate, head-first dive which brought my fingertips on the flag. I could just grab it, and over I went into the water with my mouth wide open. Though I choked and sputtered, I held onto the flag and waded happily ashore with it.

"Good for you," the minister said. "Guess you have won the . . ."

But just then two boys shouted, "She's not a Baptist! She doesn't belong!"

The minister looked surprised and cleared his throat. "Well, now, what church do you belong to?"

I had a funny feeling in my stomach as I answered in a low voice, "The Congregational Church in Saco." I knew before he spoke again that I had lost the little pig. I threw the red flag down and started running for home. I wanted to get there fast before I began to cry.

"Wait a minute!" someone shouted, but I paid no attention. I got through the village street with some sobs shaking me, but the tears didn't flood over until I reached our gate. Grandfather was standing there, and he listened quietly while I told him what had happened. "Pshaw now," he said, shaking his head. "Come with me."

I put my wet hand into his big, warm one and stumbled beside him as he walked over to the Stewarts' barn. He led me around to the pigpen at the back. "Look here!" he said. I looked and saw three big, dirty pigs, their bristles coarse and dusty, their feet muddy and a horrid smell coming from the pen. "In just a few weeks your little pig would be like this." I knew he was right, but it didn't make me feel much better.

"Come on now," Grandfather said and, holding my hand firmly, he took me around to the barn door. Inside the big barn the high haymows were full of hay, and in the back of the barn some hay had spilled over on the floor. Grandfather guided me over to this pile of hay. Mrs. Stewart's tabby cat was lying there with three little kittens playing beside her. Two were gray and one was black. The black kitten had two white paws and a spot of white under its neck. Its little tail was pointing straight up in the air as it scrambled uncertainly over the hay.

"Mrs. Stewart wants to give away the kittens," Grandfather said, "and I told your mother we might take one. We need a mouser in the barn."

I knelt down in the hay with a sudden feeling of happiness and picked up the little black kitten. Its small, red tongue came out and lapped my fingers. As I scratched its head, it began to purr, and at that moment I forgot the pig.

Fourth of July was not over until Captain Jones' fireworks had been set off. He had collected the money for them from a few people in the village. Grandfather had given him ten dollars, we knew. We ate supper, and I set off my few remaining firecrackers while I waited impatiently for the long

July twilight to end. Then I brushed my hair and put on my white dotted Swiss muslin with the red sash, and Susan put on hers too, and we walked with Mother and Grandfather over to the Jones house.

The Jones porch was low and narrow, and stretched across the whole front of the house. It had no railing so it was comfortable for children to sit on the edge and hang their feet down over the grass. Mrs. Jones had brought out some chairs for the grownups. While we waited for Captain Jones to start, Mother passed around some fragrant-smelling Joss sticks which we lighted to keep the mosquitoes away.

Mr. Tompkins, Mr. Newcomb and Grandfather began to compare their gardens and to ask who had had garden peas for dinner. We all knew that farmers in Maine tried to have peas for dinner on the Fourth of July. It meant a farmer had an especially good garden because the peas had to be planted in April, and there was always the danger of a late frost. Grandfather had driven alone to Waterboro in April to plant his peas. We had feasted on them that noon, and Mother had made them especially delicious by mixing with them little pieces of brown, crispy fried, salt pork.

Captain Jones took his box of fireworks out to the triangle by the flagpole. They were mostly Roman candles, and we watched with wonder as the gold and green and red stars floated off into the night. He gave us children sparklers to light and wave, and I noticed the fireflies, tangled in Captain Jones' roses, were almost as bright. Mrs. Jones brought out some lemonade and ginger cookies and moved her gramophone onto a table just inside the screen door. It was the only gramophone in the village, and I admired it very much. It had a big horn, and had to be wound up by a crank on the side. Mrs. Jones let me wind it up for her. The records were black cylinders that revolved. At the start, the name of the piece was announced, followed by the words "Edison Record."

I liked "Listen to the Mocking Bird," especially the part that was whistled. Mrs. Jones played mostly patriotic songs, a "Yankee Doodle" medley, "Columbia the Gem of the Ocean" and Captain Jones' favorite, "Tenting Tonight on the Old Camp Ground." Just as Captain Jones set off a final beautiful fountain of sparks, she played this a second time, and then we said "Thank you" and started for home. I was sleepy. It had been a long day.

THIRTEEN

Haying and a Night
in the Hayloft

The field behind Grandfather's barn was one of my favorite
spots. It stretched in lovely, green waves of grass back to
the pinewoods. One small section of it near the house was
fenced in for Nellie, and the fence then ran down one side
by the road. The fence posts were granite and whitewashed
boards were wired to them in long, horizontal lines. I often
sat on the top rail of Nellie's yard and looked out over the
field and, while I fed Nellie an apple, I could watch the
ripples of wind bend the grass, making it look green as it
bowed in one direction, and then brown and gold as a little

squall tipped it another way.

Halfway down the field, beside the road, were two tall poplar trees. They looked straight and lonesome with their branches held stiffly up. Grandfather was very stern in telling us not to walk in the field when the grass was tall and almost ready to cut. He no longer called it "grass" but "hay," and the three or four tons of hay which came from the field, and were stored in the barn, were sold in the fall to help pay taxes—always, of course, saving enough for Nellie.

If I walked on the edge of the field until I reached the border of the woods, I came to a small, hollow depression that was like a green velvet bowl. There was almost no grass here, and the little hollow was lined with moss that grew about four inches high. On each tiny stalk of moss was a little bright red cap. There was moisture under the moss, and I liked to feel the springy texture of this lovely carpet. Once I lay down flat on my back on the moss, and the blue sky and some fluffy white clouds seemed very near. My hollow was surrounded by the swaying stalks of grass in the flat field above me, and they seemed like miniature trees. I watched a tiny green grasshopper trying to climb up a tall and slippery stalk. I imagined I was Gulliver in *Gulliver's Travels*.

Just before the field merged into the woods, there was a strip where the grass was thin. The coarse grass of the woods was fighting with the tender green of the field. Here grew black-eyed Susans and, tucked under a pine tree, I sometimes found a red woods lily. I was not allowed to go into the woods alone, but I might go this far, and Grandfather was glad to have the flowers picked. He called daisies "white weed" and he didn't want any flowers to mix with the good hay and spoil its flavor.

When the day arrived for the field to be cut, Henry Chadwick and his brother, George, drove up to the house as soon as the dew was dry. Behind their workcart was tied the two-wheeled mower to which their horse was soon transferred. Henry got on the springy seat of the mower while George got ready to cut the grass under the roadside bushes with his scythe. At his belt, he had tied a whet-stone about a foot long and half an inch thick. Every little while he stopped cutting and pushed his wide straw hat way back on his head while he sharpened the long curving blade of his scythe.

Henry rode the mower easily, though I wondered why he didn't bounce off. The long cutting blade stretched out to his right about six feet, and his seat moved up and down on the uneven places. He had to be quick to press the handle that lifted the blade when he came to an especially rough spot, and at the end of a row he turned the horse and the mower carefully so that the horse would not get tangled in the reins or cut by the blade. As the machine and knife turned, they made a noise like winding an enormous clock. The long swathes of green lay in even rows behind the cutter, but sometimes there was a spot where they didn't completely overlap. Grandfather was watching, holding a sharp sickle, and he would walk out into the field and cut down these ragged bunches of grass.

Henry and George brought a gallon jug of sweet water with them and put it under the apple tree by the barn. This drink was well water sweetened with molasses and cinnamon. All the farmers we knew claimed it was the best drink for satisfying their thirst when haying on a hot summer day. I marveled at the way George picked up the jug with one hand, and, holding it by its small curved handle, turned it deftly so that it rested on his forearm as he took a long drink. He told me I could try this, but I dribbled the sweet water all over my dress, and I was disappointed by the taste.

The sun was very hot, and that was just what was needed to dry the hay. Like many other farmers, George and Henry wore long woolen underclothes while working in the hot sun. I could see the sleeves of Henry's red wool undershirt stretching below his blue cotton outside shirt. The wool absorbed perspiration and was "healthy," he claimed.

I stopped watching the mowing after a while, but I had just gone into the house when George came in after me holding two little rabbits in his hands. He had almost cut them when his scythe turned over their nest. The mother had run away, but the little rabbits were too small and scared to run. They were so tiny I could hold both of them in my cupped hands. Mother lined a small box with cotton, and we put them in it with some pieces of carrots. We could see their little hearts beating from fright, but after we placed them in a quiet spot behind the kitchen stove and left them undisturbed, they began to nibble the carrots.

Hay must dry thoroughly before being stored away. By early afternoon the field was cut and Grandfather and Henry and George each took a pitchfork, and, walking through the field, spread the hay out and shook the bigger chunks apart. Grandfather called this "tedding" the hay.

Now, I could run down the center of the field if I wished, and I did this with my arms stretched wide. I pretended I was a bird flying to the woods. I noticed the sun was already changing the fresh, green smell of the grass to the more concentrated fragrance of hay.

Our hay lay drying for two days during which Grandfather often walked about the field, turning it over so the sun could reach it all. The weather was dry and hot. It was haying time for all the farmers and we could hear the distant chur-r-r of mowing machines each morning. Great loads of hay went by our house every day. The biggest wagonful was pulled by Harry Smith's oxen. The hay was piled so high that it spilled over and only the heads of the oxen showed.

Then the day came when George and Henry came back with their big haywagon and the wide two-wheeled rake with its curved iron teeth. As Henry drove the rake down the field, it skimmed the surface of the earth without digging into the soil, but sometimes it hit a rock and bounced. He drove from the barn to the woods and then crossways until the whole field was filled with heaped-up mounds of hay about four wagon lengths apart. Susan and I longed to jump in these soft piles, but Grandfather warned us not to scatter the hay, and so we waited excitedly for our own part in the next operation. We believed that we had a very important job to do.

Finally, the big haywagon was hitched up with Henry driving, and George and Grandfather walking beside it. We climbed into the wagon at the place at the back where the slats were wide and held onto the sides so as not to be jolted out. George and Grandfather filled their pitchforks and tossed the hay over the sides. It was our task to tramp it down, and we rushed from one end of the wagon to the other, trying to keep the hay from sliding out and stamping it down so there would be room for more and more. We could do this easily when Grandfather tossed his pitchforkful over the side, but George could lift an enormous amount. He would stab the pile of hay deep with his fork, then turn the fork under and pin down an even bigger pile. When he lifted it over his head, it looked as if a mountain of hay was coming at us, and when he yelled "Look out," we shrieked with excitement and scrambled away so as not to get buried.

As the hay rose higher and higher, Grandfather called to us to stay in the middle so that we would not slide off onto the ground. At last the haywagon could hold no more, the load was complete, and we sat on top of it all—breathless from our efforts and happy that we could rest on our soft seat for the ride to the barn.

The ride was all too short. Even so, everything looked strange. We were seeing the field and barn from a higher level than ever before. We had to lie flat so as not to be scraped by the top branches of the apple tree. At the barn we scrambled down and ran up the barn stairs to watch the hay come in the hayloft door. George stood in the wagon and lifted tremendous pitchforkfuls of hay that came tumbling through the door in great fragrant waves. Henry and Grandfather pitched it behind them as fast as they could.

By the time the fourth and last load came in, the hay was as high as the big beams that went across the hayloft and, though I was hot and tired, with prickly pieces of hay down my neck and in my hair, I couldn't leave the barn until I tried a few dives from the beam into the hay. I even tried falling backward off the beam, and the hay was still so loosely packed that I bounced and then settled deep into a soft bed.

Grandfather's barn was as high as the house, a big square barn with a weathervane at the peak of the roof. It was joined to the house by an ell that extended behind the main house. Downstairs in this ell and leading out of the kitchen was the woodshed, piled high with birch and pine logs for the cookstove and the fireplaces.

Over the woodshed was an unfinished room with a low slanting ceiling which was called the corn chamber. When Grandfather was a young man and had a large garden, he hung the plaited bunches of seed corn to dry in this room. At the house end of the corn chamber a door opened into Uncle Lon's bedroom, and at the other end was the door of the barn chamber or hayloft.

The hayloft and the attic were my two favorite places for reading on a rainy day. When it was hot I could push open the outside door of the barn loft, and sit on the piled-up hay near the door while the cool breeze from the lake and the mountain blew in on me. The patter of rain on the roof and the muted sound of a horse clop-clopping on the road helped carry me to the country of my book.

I thought it would be fun to sleep all night in the hayloft, but for a long time Mother would not let me try it. She said I would be frightened in the night, and the mosquitoes would bother me, but at last she consented.

I made some careful preparations. First, I made a nest near the door and spread a big patchwork quilt in it. Then I took a large cotton umbrella of Grandfather's, opened it and stuck it halfway down in the hay behind my pillow. Mother gave me some mosquito netting which I draped over the umbrella and down over my pillow.

I decided to get in my nest before it got dark, so I put on my nightgown and kimono and went out through the corn chamber with my blanket. I took some cookies with me in case I was hungry in the night, and I had three or four books, but it was getting too dark to read. To be sure no mice were around, I brought Pinkie, our cat, and fixed a special pillow for her beside me. I felt very safe and snug. The big downstairs door of the barn was shut and Nellie stamped every little while in her stall, so I didn't feel alone.

The hay was not quite as soft as I thought it would be. Outside, in the twilight, I could see two bats swooping and diving. They flapped their wings very fast and were not as graceful as swallows. Once one came in the door, but quickly went out again. The evening star was bright over the mountain, and a tree toad was trilling from the hollow between two branches of a maple beside the house.

Suddenly, it was the middle of the night, and I had been asleep a long time. The moon was shining in the hayloft door. Outside, the road looked very white and strangely empty. The maple trees made long shadows. Behind me the mounds of hay were like black velvet. Pinkie stretched, and I grabbed her so she would not run away. Then a bullfrog down at the lake went "Kerchunk," and another answered him. There was a strange acrid smell, and I knew a skunk had come to the water barrel by the side of the house for a drink. I had never seen a skunk, but sometimes I had smelled one in the night, and Grandfather had told me that the strong smell meant the skunk was frightened. I tightened my hold on Pinkie.

Way off in the distance I heard a hound baying. I guessed it belonged to the Chadwicks and suddenly his bark became quick and excited. I wondered if he was chasing a fox. Right beside me a cricket chirped. It seemed unusually loud, and when Pinkie moved it stopped.

I pushed the hay around under my back and pulled the blanket close. "Everyone in the house is asleep," I thought. The whippoorwill on the fence by the apple tree began to call. I started to count the number of times he repeated his command. "Who is Will?" I wondered, and I was asleep again.

The morning songs of the birds woke me. The mist was rising from the lake. Mr. Tompkins' rooster started to crow and way off in the distance I could hear another rooster crowing. Mr. Stewart went by driving his three cows to their pasture. I picked up my blanket and went through the corn chamber to my bedroom. For the first time I thought my own bed looked more comfortable than the haymow, but I was very proud to have slept out there the whole night through. I hurried to wake up Mother and tell her about it.

FOURTEEN

Making Ice Cream

Ice cream was a rare and wonderful treat. I think raspberry was my favorite kind and that meant waiting until Mrs. Smith, who lived a mile from our house, sent word that her raspberries were ripe and that we might come to pick some. When this happened, Susan and I each got an empty lard pail from the pantry and hurried to the Smith farm.

Mrs. Smith would be looking for us and she usually asked us to step into her big kitchen. There, standing on the table, were jars and jars of newly cooked raspberry preserve. She and her family rarely ate the fresh fruit; she preserved all they picked to use in the winter. But Susan and I had other plans and when she said heartily, "Go right out and help yourselves," we thanked her and went quickly to the raspberry patch.

Right behind the barn was a little brook that hurried down off the mountain and watered part of the Smiths' vegetable garden. The raspberry bushes were on the other side of the brook. They had once been wild but Mr. Smith had taken care of them, cutting out the dead bushes and giving the new shoots a chance to grow. Even so, they grew in a tangled mass which made them hard to pick. Their thorns were long and sharp, and honeybees buzzed all around them.

Susan and I each chose a spot where the berries seemed thickest and started to fill our pails. In some places the berries were so ripe that just as my fingertips touched them they fell off on the ground. In other spots, when I reached thoughtlessly across the bushes for some particularly large berries, I scratched my hands and arms, but, oh, how delicious they smelled! I tasted only one or two because I wanted to fill my pail quickly. Blueberries and blackberries, I knew, would fill a pail faster than raspberries because they were firmer. Ripe raspberries are soft and almost melt together, so it took a good many to fill our pails. We picked steadily for half an hour and then thanked Mrs. Smith, who said they were "wild berries anyhow" and she didn't want any money. We started for home with our pails full to the top.

Now we had to get the cream. The Tibbetts farm was in the opposite direction from the Smiths', but only half a mile away. Susan and I walked there, each of us carrying a tin milk can. The Tibbettses had six cows and Mrs. Tibbetts was famous for making butter. She was proud to tell people how many pounds she made in a year. She really did not want to sell the cream, even though she might get more money for it than for butter and would also be saved the work, but she was a friend of Mother's so we were hopeful that we could persuade her to sell us enough for our ice cream.

Mrs. Tibbetts had been a schoolteacher before her marriage and she dearly loved to read, but she owned very few books. Mother found this out one day and began asking her to stop at our house when she passed by on the way to the store. Mother gave her our magazines and often loaned her books which Mrs. Tibbetts covered with a folded brown paper to keep them clean. Then another time, Mother discovered Mrs. Tibbetts loved flowers and sometimes found a strange one in the woods behind her house. She didn't have a flower book so Mother told her to come to our house with the flower and together they shared the fun of looking up its name. And so they were good friends, and Susan and I were counting on this to help get some cream.

When we reached the Tibbetts farm we couldn't find Mrs. Tibbetts but we guessed she might be out in the barn in her milk room. Just outside the milk room, under an apple tree, there was a deep well that had brick walls and a brick curb. A big bucket on an iron chain could be lowered into the cold water and Mrs. Tibbetts sometimes kept her extra milk in a large can resting in this bucket. As we walked toward the milk room, we could hear Mrs. Tibbetts' churn and we were glad to step out of the hot sun into this cool room. The floor was made of big flat stones which Mr. Tibbetts had found in his pasture, and drooping willow trees shaded the roof.

"How about some buttermilk?" Mrs. Tibbetts called cheerfully. She opened the churn where the little chunks of butter were beginning to form and dipped out some of the rich buttermilk into two cups. We drank it slowly. She looked at our tin milk cans and knew right away what we wanted but she asked us to wait a few minutes until her butter had "come." As we waited we looked at a blue ribbon tacked to the wall and the card underneath it which said Mrs. Tibbetts had won first place at the county fair for her butter. She told us that the prize was given for the fine quality of her butter and she pointed to the mold she used for each half pound. It was made of wood with a spray of buttercups cut in the bottom.

Finally the butter did come, and Mrs. Tibbetts took a big, irregular, yellow ball out of the churn, wrapped it in a damp cloth and put it on the table. Then she turned to look at our milk cans. "Two quarts?" she asked. "Please," we said together.

Eight large round shallow pans of milk were standing on a long table nearby, and the cream had risen to the top of six of these. Mrs. Tibbetts took a thin tin skimmer and gently pushed the cream to one side of the pan. It was thick and yellow and so rich that it folded into deep creases as if it were whipped cream, only heavier. She lifted it up on her skimmer and the milk fell back through the small holes in the thin tin. Then she carefully transferred it to a pitcher and from there poured it into our milk cans. Mrs. Tibbetts shook her head regretfully but let us pay her eighty cents for the two quarts.

When we reached home, Mother had already made a custard with six or more eggs and now she blended this with the cream and the raspberries. But we had two more things to get before we could make ice cream. One was rock salt which we quickly bought at the store and the other was a big cake of ice.

By the side of the lake, just beyond the bridge, was Mr. Clough's icehouse. In the middle of winter when the ice on the lake was thick, Mr. Clough sawed out great big squares of it and pulled them up a slanting runway into the icehouse. He covered the ice with sawdust from Mr. Haskell's sawmill and it did not melt even on the hottest days.

Susan and I had a small play express cart, just big enough to hold a fifty-pound chunk of ice. Mr. Clough saw us coming and he knew what we were after. In no time he had a big piece of ice loaded in the wagon. We paid him ten cents.

Now, at last, we could start to freeze the ice cream. Mother poured the delicious-looking mixture into the metal freezer can and adjusted the dasher and the cover. She carried this out to the barn where the wooden tub of our White Mountain freezer was standing. We always froze ice cream in the barn door because we kept the ice in a tin tub out there and, besides, it was good to stand where there was likely to be a cool breeze.

Grandfather came out from the house and broke the big cake of ice into several smaller pieces with his axe. He surprised us by saying he didn't care much for ice cream. Blueberry pie was much better. Next, I dumped the ice into a gunny sack and Susan and I hammered it with a wooden mallet until it was broken into small chips. With a measuring cup, Mother poured four cupfuls of ice and then one of rock salt around the freezer can and repeated this until the wooden tub was full.

Then began the job of turning the crank. Susan and I took turns for maybe ten minutes and it wasn't hard at all, but after a while the crank began to stick. This meant the freezing of the cream had started. We both gave a shout and I poked the ice and salt down with a stick and tipped the freezer a little so that the ice water would pour out of a little hole near the bottom of the tub. Then I jammed in more ice and we began turning with fresh energy. I had to hold the cover down hard with one hand so it would not jerk off as I turned the crank with my other hand. I could only push it around about eight times, and this took all my strength, before giving it over to Susan for a few turns. We were going slower and slower, and we knew it was almost finished.

Just then Mother appeared with a big plate and several spoons. She tested the hardness of the ice cream by turning the crank around once. She nodded and told us it was frozen hard. Next she carefully wiped the top of the freezer can so that no ice or salt would fall inside when she removed the cover. Then, while we watched eagerly, she took the cover off. There was the delicious, rosy cream, in all its lovely folds, which we had worked so hard to make. We could hardly wait to taste it. Mother pushed the ice cream down with her big spoon and gently pulled the dasher out. We begged her to leave plenty of ice cream on it, for eating the ice cream on the dasher was the reward for turning the crank.

Mother put the dasher on the big plate and handed it to me. It was still covered with a generous amount of ice cream and Susan and I quickly sat down side by side on the grass outside the barn door. We were hot and tired but we forgot all that as the cold velvety blend of sweet ripe raspberries and rich cream slipped down our throats.

FIFTEEN

Sunday

Susan and I thought our Sundays at Waterboro Center were very long. We had been glad at first that Grandfather considered it too hard on Nellie to drive her eight miles to the Congregational Church in Alfred, but we soon discovered there was very little we could do to make the day pass quickly. It never occurred to us to go swimming or rowing or jumping in the hay. This would be against Sunday rules. Mother read Bible stories to us to make up for not going to church and we went for quiet walks in the woods but I often missed the pleasant, ordered routine of Sundays in the winter in Saco.

The mill bells in Saco rang at 6:00 A.M. every morning

except Sunday. There was one on each of the big cotton factories down by the river, and they clanged together harshly and rapidly. I thought they said, "Get to work! Get to work!" I was glad they were not calling me and that I could turn over and sleep for another half hour before I must hop up and get ready for school.

The church bells on Sunday had a sweeter tone and were pulled more gently. I liked to hear them and I knew the deep, distant bell was at the Baptist Church and the high, clear bell was on the tall steeple of our own Congregational Church. Susan and I were sometimes eating breakfast when the nine o'clock church bell rang, though, of course, Grandfather and Mother had finished theirs long before. It was the only morning we were allowed to be late.

On getting up, I took my Sunday bath in the long tin tub in the bathroom. The room was sheathed with narrow, matched boards stained dark brown, and the slippery, tin tub was also encased in brown boards. The bathroom was dark and not very warm, and I enjoyed lying under the hot, soapy water as long as possible. I felt as if my body was melting away and my toes seemed a great distance from my head. When Mother called me, I hastily rubbed myself dry and dressed in the clean clothes she had laid out. First, there was my long winter underwear that was a little stiff and had shrunken a bit from being washed many times. I wiggled into it and the warmth of my body soon made it soft and tight-fitting. I had to smooth the long legs of the drawers carefully around my ankles and under my black stockings. Then came my Ferris waist, which buttoned down the front, and always seemed to have more buttons than I could possibly use. My chemise followed and my heavy cotton petticoat which buttoned around my waist. My Sunday dress was dark blue serge and, though it felt itchy, I thought it was very pretty. It had a wide, white lace collar which Mother had crocheted, and the sleeves were long and puffed out above the elbow. The skirt was trimmed at the bottom with three rows of *soutache* braid. I was very proud of my Sunday boots, which were black patent leather with cloth tops that buttoned with little round black buttons. The cloth fitted tightly over my instep and I had to use a buttonhook to pull the buttons through the buttonholes. I put on a big, white apron with long sleeves over my Sunday dress while I ate breakfast.

Sunday breakfast consisted of Saturday supper baked beans which had been kept warm all night on the back of the big iron stove in the kitchen. They had a rich, delicious flavor and the brown bread, which had been toasted in the oven, was thick and moist, and the melted butter filled up all the tiny holes. On the edges the crust was brown and crunchy. Some of Mother's piccalilli went with this, and it was my favorite breakfast.

On cold winter mornings Grandfather had a fire burning in the open Franklin stove in the dining room, and while we ate breakfast Mother sat near it looking over the Sunday school lesson she was going to teach after church.

The nine o'clock church bell was followed by one at ten and another at ten-fifteen. With this third bell we could see people coming from their houses up and down the street.

As we joined them Mother said a quiet "Good morning" to our neighbors, and they answered in their Sunday voices.

The First Congregational Church which Mother had attended as a little girl was in the square below our house. Standing at our gate, I could look through the high arches of the elm trees and see it facing me. The elms were very old, their thick trunks crowded the sidewalk, and in many places the bricks of the sidewalk had been pushed up by their strong roots. When Tim Cassidy ploughed the snow, it piled up in great heaps beside the biggest elms, making the path narrow, and Mother had to hold up her long skirt with one hand so as not to get the ruffle wet with snow. She wore a snug-fitting, black sealskin coat and carried a small round sealskin muff. I loved to smooth the soft fur of her coat, but I usually tried to walk a few steps behind her as I went to church so that the long black crepe veil of her widow's cap would not blow against me. It made me shiver, and I thought the weight of the veil pulled back Mother's fine, light brown hair uncomfortably.

On weekdays I liked to play a tune with a stick on the fences on our street. Grandfather's ornate iron fence made a fine ringing noise. The Simpsons' house next door had a white picket fence, and the Chases beyond that had round wooden rungs. Then came an uninteresting fence of flat, horizontal white boards which I only touched lightly because Mr. Fletcher, who lived there, would come out and look very cross.

On Sundays I didn't play a tune but walked along quietly with maybe an occasional hop and skip where the sidewalk was especially uneven.

The Congregational Church was a comforting place. I liked the red cushions and the windows of clear glass above the side balconies through which I could see the tops of the elms. Father did not seem so far away here and, looking out the window at the sky, I imagined I was in that other white church in Biddeford where he had been the minister.

It was hard to sit quietly by Mother and pay attention to what was being said in the high pulpit way up at the front of the church. Mother seemed to know this and sometimes she would put her hand gently over mine. This reminded me to listen for the text of the sermon which I would be asked to repeat to Grandfather when we got home.

I kept my eyes tightly shut during the prayers. Ever since I had been a very little girl, I believed that angels came down from Heaven to carry the minister's prayers up to God. I thought they would disappear if I opened my eyes and, though I soon knew the angels were not truly visible, I liked to pretend they were, and I shut my eyes as tight as I could.

When it was time to sing the last hymn, it felt good to stand up. I now could twist my head around and look at the organ in the balcony. Mr. Shannon, the organist, was a little man with quantities of white hair that curled on his neck. He bowed way over the keys when playing. Though I liked to hear the music, I was more interested in watching Jimmy MacIntire who stood in a little recess beside the organ and pumped a long wooden handle of the bellows up and down. It was hard work, and he couldn't rest for a moment or the organ would stop playing.

When Mother, Susan and I walked home after Sunday school we each carried a book from the Sunday school library. The Little Colonel books were my favorites and I was glad Sunday was a day when I could read the whole afternoon through. I knew it was wicked to go sliding on Sunday or to play hide-and-seek in the barn; but I could read as much as I wished and this made me happy.

Our Sunday dinner was oyster stew. Among the oysters we sometimes found tiny pink crabs about half as big as a ten-cent piece. Hunting for these was the only surprise about this meal, which was invariably stew, pear preserve and marble cake.

After dinner we went into the sitting room. The room had a friendly, well-worn feeling that seemed to close around me and make me feel secure and safe. On the floor was a Brussels carpet with a pattern of faded roses. Grandmother had bought it right after she and Grandfather were married, and he couldn't see any reason why Mother should want to replace it with a newer one. The fireplace was shallow, but a black iron fireframe with shining brass knobs on either corner jutted into the room and threw out the heat. On Sunday afternoons in winter a fire was usually burning. The afternoon sun streamed in the two windows that looked out on the yard. Between them stood a large Victorian sofa upholstered with black horsehair, and Susan liked to sit there. There was a low slipper rocker that matched the sofa, and Mother would pull this close to the fire and occasionally push the logs together with the poker when she looked up from her book. The Morris chair was my place. Its cushions were covered with brown corduroy and it stood in one of the windows. I liked to sit on the arm with my feet in the seat. Strangely enough, Mother did not seem to mind. Mother, Susan and I lost ourselves in our books and hardly spoke to one another. Sometimes I got an apple from the barrel in the barn and munched it as I read. Sometimes, as a special treat, Mother thought it would not break the Sunday rules if we popped some corn over the fire.

Up in our attic was a small closet filled with newspapers and old magazines. Some Sunday afternoons, when my book was exciting and I didn't want to be interrupted, I went upstairs to this closet and sat on the floor to read. Mother had told me that she used to hide there to read when she was little because Grandfather did not approve of her reading as much as she liked to. When I sat in the closet, I kept the door wide open, and the light came down on my book from the skylight in the ceiling.

My father's rolltop desk was stored in the attic and on top of it was the brown, stuffed owl which had stood there when the desk was in the study in the Biddeford parsonage. I liked to put my book on his desk and think back to when I was a very little girl and Father allowed me to sit in the bottom drawer of the desk while he wrote his sermons. I remembered how he had walked up and down the study holding his sermon in front of him and reciting parts of it. I used to walk behind him waving a piece of paper which I called my sermon.

There were some Sundays when we children found we had chosen books that did not hold our interest and, when

Mother realized this, she suggested that we go into the parlor with her to look at her albums of photographs. In the parlor was Mother's tea table, a high, round mahogany table on which was an embroidered linen cloth and six Dresden cups and saucers. In each saucer was a silver spoon and each of these came from a different city. The one I liked best was from Paris, and the handle was an orchestra leader holding his baton in his raised hand. In the center of the table was a silver teapot with an alcohol lamp under it which was lighted when some of Mother's friends came to tea.

There were heavy lace curtains in the parlor and the sofa was upholstered in yellow satin. Mother would let us sit on either side of her on the sofa while she explained the pictures of London and Paris and Vienna which she had collected, and told us about the winter she had spent in Vienna while Uncle Byron was studying medicine. (It was exciting to hear of Mother's waltzing with Austrian officers who whirled her around so rapidly that she almost lost her breath.)

But I liked the stereopticon pictures better than the flat photographs, and I was sometimes allowed to carry the box containing them out of the parlor to a place where I could look at them all by myself. Our hall had a winding staircase and at the top a balcony curved all the way around the stairwell. There was a high ladderback chair with a rush seat in a sunny window of the balcony and, if I sat there and pressed the glass of the stereopticon viewer tightly against my face, I could step right into a leafy forest or watch the water of Niagara Falls foam and tumble straight at me.

I had discovered, too, that my seat by the window in the balcony was a wonderful place from which to watch the fast horses that pulled sleighs down our snowy street. At other times, I turned my chair toward the stairwell and pretended I was in the gallery of a theatre. Halfway down the curve of the staircase was a niche where a marble bust of Augustus Caesar stood. He seemed to be sitting in a theatre, too. The light in the lower hall was dim, and I could just barely see the dark, mahogany grandfather's clock that spoke a slow, gentle tick-tock, tick-tock. On the wall, facing the foot of the stairs, was a large plaque of light wood with the outline of a knight in armor burned into it. Above it were two crossed swords. This knight guarded our front door.

One particular Sunday I was sick with a sore throat. I had played too long in the snow on Saturday, and I was glad to be sent upstairs in the early evening to my big, comfortable bed. It was a heavy, dark oak bed with a high headboard. Stiffly starched, lace-trimmed pillow shams were over the pillows, and these I draped on a chair. The straw matting on the floor was cold so I quickly got into bed while Mother lighted the fire in the fireplace across the room. Then she got ready her favorite remedy for a sore throat which was antiphlogiston, a sticky salve that has the texture and appearance of putty. She got a long strip of white flannel about four inches wide and with a silver knife spread it thickly with this salve. She lighted the kerosene lamp that stood on my bureau and wrapped the dry side of the flannel around the glass chimney. The heat of the lamp came through and the salve glistened as it got hot. I watched fearfully, dreading the mo-

ment when the bandage would go around my neck and wondering if I would get burned, but it was just comfortably
warm.

Susan came in and sat on the bottom of the bed with a
quilt around her shoulders, and Mother pulled her chair
close to the lamp and read *Pilgrim's Progress*. Long after she
blew out the lamp, the flickering shadows of the fire on the
ceiling looked like Christian carrying his heavy burden. With
the last glimmer of the fire, I thought I saw Christian throw
his load away and I was greatly relieved.

One summer we got what Grandfather called a big dose
of religion. A Baptist revivalist came to Waterboro Center
and there was a meeting every night of the week in the town
hall. Many people in our village went to hear him, some of
them because there wasn't much to do on a summer night.
Mother thought we should go because we had not been to
any church for several weeks. Mr. Richards had six singers
with him who sang "Bringing in the Sheaves" and "Though
your sins be as scarlet they shall be as white as snow." I
thought these were lovely songs. I soon knew them by heart,
and I sang them joyfully at home until Grandfather said,
"Do you really know what you are singing about?" I thought
I did. The part about sin did not concern me, but I liked "We
shall come rejoicing bringing in the sheaves," and I hummed
it to myself as I picked stringbeans.

Then, after two days of quiet preaching about the Bible
and of training a chorus to sing, Mr. Richards began to talk
about Hell. He was a tall thin man with very black eyebrows

and he spoke in a deep voice, pointing his finger at different people in the room. I had never heard much about Hell before, though I felt pretty well acquainted with Heaven. In my Sunday school book was a picture of a kind old gentleman with a long white beard looking through the clouds in the sky. This was God, and He was just above us in Heaven. But now there was somebody else to think about—the Devil. All at once I began to feel afraid as Mr. Richards shouted that we all might go to Hell. After this third meeting, Mother said she didn't think we needed to go any more, but I persuaded her to let me go with Mrs. Jones. I guess Mother thought I wanted to hear the music, but I really wanted to hear more about Hell.

By the fifth meeting, the hall was crowded with people who had come from the neighboring farms and many teams were hitched to the fence rail out back. Inside, as Mr. Richards described Hell, everyone was very quiet. Mrs. Jones, sitting beside me, kept picking the material of her dress and clearing her throat.

The town hall was lighted by kerosene lamps set in brackets along the side walls. Black cotton netting was tacked across the open windows to keep the bugs out, but some moth millers got inside the room and flew repeatedly against the lamp chimneys until they got burned and fell down. I couldn't help watching them as Mr. Richards preached about Hell. I wanted desperately to be good because I felt it would help Mother, but when Mr. Richards said it was wicked to be thoughtless and careless, I remembered with a sinking feeling how I had slid down the stair bannisters in the front hall in Saco that spring and had hit a table, knocking over and smashing Mother's favorite Dresden vase.

When he talked about selfishness that was even worse. Only the week before the preaching mission started, Mother had given me five cents for weeding the garden, and when she handed me the money I said that I wished, for once, I could buy some candy and eat it all myself without passing it around. "Very well, you may," Mother said. I ran over to the store and bought five luscious, big chocolate creams. It was my very favorite candy. The first one seemed to fill the whole of me with a satisfying, delicious sensation, and I ate it as fast as I could. The second one I started to eat with little, tiny bites . . . But suddenly I didn't want it at all. I tried to give one to Mother, but she shook her head and insisted they were all for me. By the time I bit into the third one I was very unhappy, and I thought I would choke if I took another bite. I ran down to the blacksmith shop and left the last two on Mr. Sawyer's workbench, and I knew I was very selfish.

As the week went on Mr. Richards preached more and more about Hell. One night I dreamed that I was running down a long, long road and that I fell into a slough of despond like Christian and my best dress was all covered with mud.

Mr. Richards' mission was to end on a Saturday and on that day he planned to baptize in the lake all those who wanted their sins washed away. In the store that Saturday morning I met Suzy Abbot who lived a little way down the road. She was jumping up and down with excitement and said, "I'm going to be baptized! I'm going to wear my best white dress and wade right into the water with it on. Are you going to be baptized? You'll go to Hell if you aren't baptized."

I shook my head, but I was very distressed because I somehow knew that Mother did not approve of Mr. Richards' kind of preaching, and yet I wanted to be saved. If I could only be baptized it would be easy to be good.

After dinner that Sunday I went quickly upstairs and put on my white dress. I came down the back stairs and went out through the barn so that no one would see me, and then I ran as fast as I could to the lake. Mr. Richards had placed a small portable organ on the sand near our boathouse. The choir, which now had many people in it, was singing "Throw Out the Life Line," and it seemed to me the bank of the lake was crowded with people. I got behind the big pine tree beside our boathouse and looked through the thick, low branches. Mr. Richards was wearing a black robe and was carrying a long staff. He walked out into the water up to his waist and planted the staff. Then he came back to the shore and called for all unbaptized persons to step forward. Slowly, one person after another came to the edge of the water and walked out with him. I saw Peleg Gooch and Mrs. Jones move up. Mr. Richards ducked each one completely under, but so quickly no one choked. Finally he came to the children and I saw Suzy going bravely into the water.

I felt I must go. I jerked off my hair ribbon and put it on one of the branches of the pine. My neck was hot and prickly under my braids. I looked around and saw that Mother and

Susan had come down to the lake and were standing behind the people sitting on the bank. Suddenly, I knew I couldn't go directly down to Mr. Richards without telling Mother first.

"Please, Mother," I said, all out of breath, "I want to be baptized."

"Hush, dear." Mother put her arm around me, holding me back.

"But I must be baptized, or I won't go to Heaven!" I said, struggling with my tears.

"I think you will surely go to Heaven," Mother said, looking at me firmly with her kind, loving smile. "You were baptized by your father when you were a baby. You don't need to be baptized again."

Suddenly I felt very happy—as if I had lost a load off my back, just as Christian did in *Pilgrim's Progress*. Suzy came by me with a blanket wrapped around her and walked over to her mother. She looked at me and I looked back, standing as straight and tall as I could in my white dress.

"I have been baptized!" I shouted, forgetting the people around me. "I was baptized by my father long, long ago!"

SIXTEEN

The Forest Fire

In August, when the woods were dry and the air was hot, we could sometimes see a faint, wispy veil of gray smoke above the horizon. It might have been many miles away but the almost imperceptible smell and the thin gray streak in the sky would make Grandfather shake his head and mutter about the waste of good timber. "Lumbermen in Maine don't clean up the woods," he grumbled. Anyone riding around the country roads could see high piles of sawdust and big heaps of slash which they had left behind. It was "terrible easy" to start a fire.

One morning Grandfather went down to Marsh's for the mail and I ran out to meet him as he returned. He stopped by one of the maple trees and looked for a few moments at the wooded ridge which ran up toward the mountain. I looked, too, and could see a small, black cloud that seemed to rise up and then sink down and then puff up a little higher and spread out like a big, fat cigar. "Looks like the blueberry plains are on fire," he said. He put the mail in my hands, turned and started quickly back to the store.

The blueberry plains were over by Scratches' Corner where, some years earlier, the timber had been cut off and the underbrush burned. Low bush blueberries had grown up in great quantities and it was said a person could pick fifty quarts or more in a day if he stripped the berries off the branches without paying too much attention to leaves that might be mixed in with them. Some farm families, after haying season, made a daylong trip there and the Foster family with their five boys usually put up a tent and stayed for several days. I loved to pick blueberries. They looked so pretty among the green leaves and they tasted so good in Mother's blueberry muffins. We could pick all we needed in the fields near the house, but it would be exciting to pick an enormous pail full. Grandfather once said he would take us over to the blueberry plains, but it was nine miles away and quite a trip for Nellie, so we had never gone.

When Grandfather came back to the house, he told us that Marsh had talked with Len Doughty who had driven the mail stage through earlier that morning. The route the stage took passed within three miles of Scratches' Corner and though Len could see that there was a heavy fire, he thought it could be stopped. There were already over thirty men fight-

ing the fire. Anyway, there was a fairly wide dirt road between the fire and the wooded ridge opposite us.

Marsh's telephone line went part way up to Limerick and
had some twenty people on it. I had often seen Marsh with
the receiver at his ear just listening to what was going on.
This morning he had already listened in and hadn't heard
of anyone being especially alarmed, though most of the
men up that way had stopped haying and were at the fire.

This did not entirely reassure Grandfather, who took the
Farmers' Almanac off the hook by the fireplace, where it
was always hung, and looked to see what the chances were
for thunderstorms. As the day went on and the dark cloud
grew larger on the horizon, he went back and forth to the
store. In the middle of the morning he even sent me over
to ask if there was any news. When I came back and said,
"Marsh says there is no news," he was not satisfied and went
over himself a few minutes later. At dinner he told us there
were now about fifty men fighting the fire and he wished
he were younger—he would go too.

At a time like this when Grandfather was uneasy and upset, it was Mother who spoke up and decided what we
should do. First of all she thought Grandfather should go
across the way to Captain Jones' house and make a plan with
him for getting everyone out of the village if it should be
necessary. There were several old people without horses and
carriages, like Mrs. MacIntire who was lame and the Widow
Hobbs who had been sick lately. Then Mother got out the
extension valise and left it open in her bedroom so that it
would be easy to pack it quickly. All the time she seemed

so cheerful and undisturbed that we children only half sensed that this was a dangerous fire. We saw two buckboards pass the house filled with men holding spades and brooms and Susan and I thought they could take care of everything. Besides, there had been other summers when wood smoke hung over the hills.

But when I asked Mother if she would take Susan and me for a swim, she said she thought it would be better if we stayed near the house in case there was further news about the fire. Susan and I were startled by this thought and looked at Mother with surprise. Suddenly we both had the same idea and started to race for the barn. Usually I could beat Susan but this time we were close together. We clattered up the stairs to the loft where the great mounds of sweet hay were stored. We tumbled on the soft heaps and threw great armfuls at each other and shouted a little louder than usual as we walked the beams, balancing for a moment before diving onto a cushion of hay. We shook the fear out of ourselves, and I was glad that the dusty brown walls of the barn prevented me from seeing that strange, dark sky.

That night we knew the fire was still spreading. The sky was red all along the ridge and behind the top of the mountain. The fire was at least nine miles away and it had not crossed the road, but it was now burning on a wider front. I thought of the big red fire engine in Saco, pulled by strong gray horses that could race so fast down the street to a fire. I wished it was in Waterboro now, but Mother told me that a fire engine could not reach a forest fire and the men had to use brooms and spades to beat it out and dig trenches, hoping the fire would not cross over.

Captain Jones came over to tell Grandfather and Mother that several families were driving off to stay with relatives some miles away. He said Peleg Gooch was going to stay in his little cabin by the lake. If the fire came down to the lake he intended to wade in up to his neck and duck his head under the water when it got hot. Captain Jones had advised him to take his old punt and row out to the middle of the lake. It seemed to me that would be a much more wonderful thing to do. I wished we could do the same.

Mr. Newcomb had no intention of leaving. He had been ploughing his pasture all afternoon and soon would have a wide strip of freshly turned earth between the fire and his house. But Miss Elvira and Miss Eleanor were nervous about staying and had packed some of their best china and the pictures of Governor Wentworth into their buggy. Captain Jones had warned them not to wait too long before deciding what they would do.

Jim Waters had started walking to Bar Mills at noon, driving his large herd of cows before him. Pete Branch, a German farmer who lived at the far end of the village, nearest the mountain, wanted to start a back fire in his big field. Captain Jones had told him it was much too dangerous but Grandfather said it might be a very good idea if the wind died down a little. All the men for miles around were at the fire and some of them would come back in time to move their families and to give a warning.

Captain Jones told Grandfather that he was going to stay up all night. He wanted to borrow Grandfather's big brass bell and planned to ring it by the flagpole if the fire got dangerously near. Grandfather thought Captain Jones was telling everyone what to do as if he were still a captain in the army.

I think Mother intended to stay up all night too, but she didn't say so. She seemed calm and unconcerned so Susan and I put "Please take care of the firefighters" in our prayers and went to bed with only a slight feeling of fear.

I woke early the next morning feeling choked by the heavy smell of smoke. My eyes smarted and I jumped quickly out of bed. And then I heard a loud hammering on one of the maple trees outside. Without waiting to dress, I ran downstairs and Mother hurried with me to the front door. High up in the maple, at a spot where a large branch had broken off in a windstorm the year before, were two giant woodpeckers. They were many times bigger than the downy woodpeckers we knew so well. Their feathers were black and straggly, their necks thin and their beaks sharp and long. On the tops of their heads were ragged red crests. They were digging the ants out of the hole in the tree.

"Pileated woodpeckers!" Mother exclaimed. "What a wonderful chance to see them!" Then she added, "They only live in the deep woods. They must have been driven out by the fire." I stood close to her twisting my nightgown with excitement, and looked with awe at these strange, powerful birds that we had never seen before. Their beaks hit the tree with such force that they seemed angry and cruel.

I raced upstairs to get dressed and right after breakfast which we all ate hastily, Grandfather said he was going to hitch up Nellie. Susan and I washed the dishes faster than we ever had, and Mother started to count the silver spoons. Every summer she carried the spoons back and forth from Saco to Waterboro and she was always especially careful of a set of twelve with pretty, ornamental handles and names engraved in the bowls. They had been a wedding present from twelve ministers in Biddeford who were friends of Father's and the name of each one was on a spoon.

As she wrapped up the spoons, Mother told us to go outside and look for Pinkie and then to sit on the front steps until she called us. Susan came over quickly to me and put her hand in mine. I held on to it tightly, partly to comfort her, but more to help myself feel brave. We walked out the front door together. As I looked around, I had a strange sensation that was half fear and half excitement. Our familiar, happy outdoor world had become dangerous. The color of the sky was yellow and it made the grass look a strange, bright green. The pink roses by the door were orange. Once in a while a tiny piece of blackened leaf fluttered down.

We didn't have to look for Pinkie. She ran up to us and jumped in Susan's arms. I looked hard at the ridge and imagined I could see flames up there even though Grandfather had said the fire was way on the other side. The fire had driven the pileated woodpeckers out, but what about the squirrels—and could the deer get away?

Across the way we could see Captain Jones packing up his wagon. I hoped he was taking his gramophone. Then Grandfather came around the corner of the house driving the surrey. He climbed down and hitched Nellie to a post of the fence. Nellie stood still but she kept switching her tail from side to side as I had never seen her do before.

Len Doughty came by with his wagon piled high with furniture. He waved his whip to us children and called to Grandfather that this was his last trip. He couldn't get back to Limerick again. He said he had to whip his horses through one section of the road where the fire was close. He had seen part of the back of the ridge and in some spots there was a crown fire, which meant the fire was jumping from treetop to treetop instead of running along the ground.

Mother and Susan and I began to pack the surrey. Grandfather spoke very little except to direct Mother about the packing. He kept his eye on the horizon and Susan and I brought things out as Mother directed and I made a special trip to collect the daguerreotypes from the parlor mantel and put them in Mother's knitting bag. We had a feeling we must hurry. The sky was getting darker.

It had been decided that we would take Widow Hobbs with us and I ran down the road to tell her we were ready. Susan and I squeezed into the front seat with Grandfather; Mrs. Hobbs, holding a pillowcase full of her things, climbed into the back seat with Mother. Grandfather made one last trip to the house and brought out the old leather-covered register. Susan and I put it across our knees. Before the Civil War the first half of this book had been an account book in Great-grandfather's store, but for the past fifty years everyone spending a night at the farm had registered in it. Grandfather had always recorded the dates on which he planted the garden in the spring and when important repairs were made to the house, such as painting it or shingling the roof. Susan's and my weight and height had been entered at the start of each summer and again when we went back to school in the fall. The births and weddings and the deaths in the family were all there.

None of us spoke as we drove away. We had a solemn feeling like being in church. I was shivering and both Susan and I wished we could sit in the back seat beside Mother. She was the only one who could make this dreadful day less bewildering.

We were told we were on our way to the Barnes place on the other side of the river. It was halfway to Saco and we might possibly go on to Saco depending on the fire. Grandfather spoke as if we were just trying to get away from the heavy smoke that hurt our throats and eyes. He didn't say that the farm might be burned, but that was in our thoughts. I was afraid to look back and yet I had to turn around to catch what might be a last look at the big barn, so unusually white against the dark sky.

We were all thankful that Nellie was trotting fast. Other people were leaving the village and some with faster horses went by us. We caught up with George Chadwick who was driving a haywagon filled with boxes and furniture. He couldn't go very fast because his two cows were hitched on behind. Grandfather came out of his thoughts to call, "You've got plenty of time."

Susan and I were glad to be going to the Barnes farm because Carrie lived there. For three years, when Susan was little, and before we came to live with Grandfather, Carrie had been our nurse and we loved her dearly. She was a young farmgirl with rosy cheeks and a hearty laugh and she had spent many hours playing games with us though, maybe, Mother would have liked it better if she had done more housework.

When we finally drove into the Barneses' yard, Carrie ran out to welcome us. Somehow she knew we were on the verge of tears. She put up her strong arms and caught each of us as we jumped out and, taking us by the hand, she led us into the kitchen while her father helped the grownups. She gave us glasses of milk and cookies and while we ate she repeated over and over, "I've got something to show you, a surprise!"

In a few minutes we felt much better and Carrie led us out to the big barn, past the haymows to the last stall. There stood a little tan calf on wobbly legs banging its head against its mother's milkbag. It looked at us with big brown eyes and put out its red moist tongue. We had to laugh. "Just born yesterday," Carrie said.

For the next two days we stayed at the Barnes farm. Carrie played with us constantly, taking us down to the brook to see the bright red cardinal flowers that were just beginning to blossom at the edge of the woods, helping us stand on the top rail of the fence and get on the broad back of her father's big farmhorse, and then leading the horse around the farmyard while I held the bridle and Susan clung tightly to my waist. She took us to the barn in the late afternoon when the four Jersey cows came in from the pasture to be milked and even let me try to pull the teats of the gentlest cow to get the milk. How she laughed when none came, but she quickly said, "Hold out your cups," and expertly squirted the milk into the tin cups Susan and I had brought from the kitchen. Whenever Carrie saw that Susan and I were worrying about our farm, she was ready with a quick game of hide-and-seek.

Grandfather drove partway back to Waterboro Center after the first night and returned with good news. Many more men had joined the firefighters and the fire had not yet come down to the village.

The next day Mr. Sawyer came by to tell us the best news of all. The danger was over. One fork of the fire had come down near the upper end of the lake and had burned out at the water's edge. He assured us that he had heard that Aunt Minnie, who lived by the old mill, was safe. Pete Branch, in spite of everyone's fears, had burned over his big field. Two or three men had been so angry with him that they thought the county sheriff should arrest him, but they were too busy taking care of their own places to stop him. When the other big fork of the fire swept over the ridge, the firefighters could not stop it, but when the flames reached Pete's blackened field it could go no further. More than a hundred men had fought the fire day and night until it was under control and nearly out. But groups of men had to watch for some time because there was fire underground in the pitchy roots of the pine trees.

We started back to Waterboro that afternoon. All the way back we greeted the familiar landmarks with new eyes. How big Grandfather's woodlot seemed and I thought the trees looked very tall. The field, which had been cut two weeks before, was smooth and beautifully green. The big barn and the dear house seemed like friends we were seeing again after a very long time.

We wondered if the house would be unchanged as we stepped through the front door. But there was Susan's doll lying on the sofa in the sitting room and the tall grandfather's clock in the corner was ticking with its usual authority. In the kitchen the water in the dishpan had not been poured out and on the table was a plate half filled with the toast Mother had made for our last breakfast.

Grandfather brought in the register and sat down at once to write a note about the fire. Mother passed a broom to Susan and me. There was a little catch in her voice as she said, "Come, let's sweep the soot off the front steps."

SEVENTEEN

Peleg Gooch

Peleg Gooch had a hare lip. It made his speech blur as if he had a hot potato in his mouth. He lived alone in a tumble-down shack by the lake, and we children had been warned by Grandfather not to have anything to do with him. We didn't understand why because he had been very kind to us; at least, he helped us when we went fishing.

Our lake was fed by springs, and the fish in it were pickerel and perch and horn pout. The numerous sunfish didn't count because they were not good to eat, and we always threw them back in the water if we caught any. At the end of the lake, the road from the village went over a bridge and on one side of it was the main lake, and on the other a swampy place where the water lay stagnant and seeped away into the rushes. The best fishing for those who stayed on the shore and didn't try for pickerel in a boat was on this bridge, and the best time to fish was toward evening.

Peleg Gooch had the longest fishing pole we had ever seen. It was cut from an ash tree, and stretched out into the water twice as far as our poles which were made from alder branches. For many hours every day he stood silently by the bridge resting his pole on the railing and vigorously chewing tobacco. Occasionally, he would spit in the water.

Susan and I loved to go fishing. We got worms from the moist earth at the end of the wooden trough which lead from the pump in our kitchen to Grandfather's garden. We used poles which Grandfather had cut and string which Mother gave us. The hooks were two for a penny at the store.

We did not feel we were disobeying Grandfather's injunction if we fished on the opposite side of the bridge from Peleg. But sometimes I would give a quick jerk to my line, and it would soar over my head and get snarled in the low branches of the maple by the bridge. I would jerk and tug and then Peleg would lean his pole on the rail of the bridge and come over to my side. "Eathy doth it!" he would say, and with a careful motion up and around, he would untangle a hopeless snarl.

There were numerous horn pout by the swampy side of the bridge, and they could be attracted by the light of a lantern. Occasionally, in the evening, when Mr. Sawyer, or one of the village boys we knew, was going for horn pout, Mother would let us go too. Several people would be standing on the bridge with their poles resting on the rail. The lantern flickered on a big granite stone that was one of the supports of the bridge. The reflection of the light in the water, the dark shadows of the trees, and the soft lap, lap of the water on the stones gave me little shivers of excitement. If I pulled in a horn pout I put my foot on it while I got out the hook because the wicked horn, or spike, on its head could cut my hand.

One time my line felt very heavy, and when I got it in I saw I had hooked an eel. I didn't know what to do. It wiggled and thrashed around, and I thought I would have to cut my line, but Peleg came over from the other side of the bridge.

"Thems good eating," he said, and deftly unhooked the eel and put it in the tin pail he was using for his catch.

Peleg's father had died when he was a little boy. The Widow Gooch owned a small house near the lake and took in washing. We used to put our wash in a big basket and wheel it down to her house in a play express wagon. She had gradually sold off her property on the shorefront, as she considered its only value was in the pine trees that might make good lumber. When she died there was nothing left for Peleg but the little shack on the shore.

Peleg had gone through the fourth grade, and then stopped. No one was sure whether he was stupid or just lazy. The men at the store didn't think much of him and were contemptuous when, in the winter, he sometimes asked the selectmen for help with his grocery bill. He was smart at tracking deer, though, and every fall he shot a big buck which furnished him with meat for a long time. In the summer he helped farmers with their haying, though he never worked for a long stretch; but early and late he could be seen going down the road with his long fishpole over his shoulder. Though he was a tall man, he kept his head down and rarely spoke. Perhaps he thought people would laugh at his strange speech.

The doors of our house were seldom locked, and several times Peleg startled us by quietly walking into the kitchen and sitting down without saying a word. Mother would kindly ask him how he was, and he would say, "Good, good" and then sit silently watching us. Grandfather would say to Mother the next day, "Send that fellow home if he comes around again"—but Mother never did.

A fire in the country is a dreadful thing, especially if water is scarce. In Waterboro there was no fire department, but if a fire started in anyone's house, all the neighbors hurried to help.

It was a hot July afternoon when the Holmes barn burned. I was out by our gate when I heard someone shouting and saw a strange cloud of black smoke coming from the Holmes place which was a little beyond the lake.

The men who were loafing at the store started to run down the road. Mr. Tompkins, who had just driven to the store to get some grain, wheeled his wagon around and two men jumped in the back as he pulled sharply on the reins and touched his horse with a whip. I forgot to ask Mother and started running through the field behind the blacksmith shop.

When I reached the Holmes place, little red curls of fire

were running up the shingles on the barn roof. The house was a little distance from the barn, but the wind was blowing in that direction. I stood with a group of children watching—and so scared I couldn't move. Two men had gone into the barn and they came out leading the horses. I could see that one of the men was Peleg, and he was stroking the nose of a brown horse that was so frightened he was prancing sideways. Peleg seemed to be talking to him as he led him over to one of the boys.

Out in the barnyard was a pump. The men formed a line and passed buckets of water from hand to hand. At first they dashed the water on the barn, but as the hay in the barn began to burn briskly it was plain that the building could not be saved. By now the shingles on the roof of the house on the side toward the fire began to smoke. Some men started throwing water on the house while Mr. Holmes dashed into the house and began pushing out furniture.

Suddenly a voice yelled, "Thtop, thtop—wet here—here!" It was Peleg who had climbed out of an attic skylight and was straddling the roof tree. He had two big cotton quilts which he had somehow wet in the kitchen sink and he was covering the smoking shingles with the wet quilts.

The men caught on to his idea and found the water was used to much better effect this way. The hot cinders were falling around Peleg, but he slapped them off and kept yelling, "Pour it on. Pour it on," and the men who were pumping and passing the water worked harder and faster.

It was a long time before the men were sure the house was safe. Mother had come to find me, and had gone in the side door to speak to Mrs. Holmes. I followed her inside. Mrs. Holmes was standing in her parlor, holding her grand-mother's teapot in one hand and her wedding picture in the other. She had pushed her most loved furniture into the hall so that the men could take it out quickly, if necessary. It was a strange and frightening thing to stand in her parlor and feel the heat of the fire coming through the walls. When Mr. Holmes came in to say the fire was under control, he was panting from the hard work. He was soaking wet and his hands and face were black.

That evening after supper Mother, Susan and I walked down to the bridge. Peleg was in his usual place, his long pole stretching out over the water. There was a strange smell in the air from the hay that had burned in the Holmes barn. Peleg's clothes too smelled of the fire. The lake was very calm, and the swallows were skimming over the water catching bugs.

Peleg was not alone. Three men who had been up to look at the Holmes place were standing by him. One of them had his hand on Peleg's arm. Peleg's head was up, and his shoulders back. He was paying no attention to his line which was deep in the water and being pulled back and forth by what must have been a very big fish.

EIGHTEEN

My Bicycle

On my tenth birthday Mother gave me a bicycle. It was red and silver and shiny, a beautiful bicycle with a tinkling bell. It was like having wings, and I rode along so smoothly that I sometimes did not know how far I had gone from home. Twice I scared Mother by riding too far and I almost had my bicycle taken away for good by Grandfather.

The first time was in Saco, I had just learned to pump the pedals fast enough so that I could take my hands off the handlebars without swerving to the side. One Saturday, in late April, Mother gave me permission to ride to Marion Blackwell's house which was down by the cemetery on the Old Orchard Road. Marion and I were going to make May baskets together. Mother had shown me how to cut colored tissue paper into a little fringe to put around a small cardboard box, and Marion's mother had taught her to make fudge, though it didn't always get hard. We had plans for making seven or eight baskets and filling them with fudge and leaving them at the front doors of school friends on May Day night. Susan was going to come with us and she had been busy for a week pasting crepe paper petals around some paper cups to make little baskets that looked like tulips. This was the first year Mother had said I might go out at night to hang May baskets and Susan could only go if we stayed together. The most fun came from putting the May baskets quietly at a door, ringing the bell and running as fast as possible, and I was a little worried that Susan might not be able to keep up.

I was thinking about all this as I rode along, using the sidewalk when no one was walking on it, but most of the time riding at the side of the street where the dirt was packed down hard. Very few teams passed me and I could take my hands off the handlebars often. Sometimes I even folded my arms daringly, as I had seen big boys do. I was feeling so carefree and happy that it was a big disappointment to find that Marion had not understood I was coming and was not at home.

The city sidewalk ended at the cemetery and the road and a hard-packed dirt path led down to the ocean three miles away. My afternoon was free, I thought, and why not ride a little distance down this inviting way? The path was level and every now and then I took my feet off the pedals and coasted. The cool April air made my hands and face cold but it was a day that sparkled all over.

When I came to some pine woods, I thought I ought to hunt for some arbutus to put on the top of our May baskets, but after that I must quickly turn around and ride home. I left my bicycle on the side of the road and went a little way under the trees. These were woods I didn't know and they seemed very strange to me. Perhaps it was because it was so still. There was none of the soft movement of birds and insects that I knew in the summer woods. In one spot there was a little patch of dirty snow where a big drift must have melted down. Last year's ferns lay flat on the ground, but in many places they had not lost their shapes but lay in tangled orange, brown masses. Beneath them I could see the furry gray tops of fiddlehead ferns sticking up for an inch or two out of the ground. In a damp hollow some big broad leaves of skunk cabbage looked surprisingly green in these gray woods. I could see a few arbutus leaves trailing along the ground in a sunny spot and I ran to them, kneeling down and pushing the leaves aside. Yes, there were a few of the tiny pink-and-white buds just starting to open. It meant spring was here and I picked them happily, holding them to my face to smell their special fragrance. Then I put them in the big pocket of my coat.

As I turned my bicycle around to ride back, I saw a bit of blue through the trees. It was deeper than the color of the sky and I knew it was the ocean. I reasoned that I really had time to go on since I had planned to stay at Marion's all afternoon. So I stood up on the pedals of my bicycle and pumped as hard as I could until even on that cool April day I felt warm and glowing. I had never seen the ocean so blue; it made me hold my breath for a minute. No one was in sight and all the summer cottages were closed. The beach was swept clean and the breakers were coming in with a slow steady swell. The white foam on top of them matched the white seagulls hovering above the water. The wide expanse of the ocean made me feel very small, and suddenly I knew I didn't belong there all by myself. If Mother had been with me I would have felt safe and protected. I would have run down on the beach to look for sand dollars and we would have laughed together as we rolled them on their edges along the smooth sand. I felt pulled in both directions, toward the beach and toward home, and I was almost in tears as I jerked my bicycle around and started back as fast as I could pedal. I was back in time for supper but the ride back had seemed very far and the long shadows of the afternoon chased me all the way home.

There was no room in the surrey to take my bicycle when Grandfather drove us to Waterboro Center in June but, a few weeks after reaching the farm, Grandfather had to return to Saco on business and since he was alone, he was able to bring the bicycle back. It seemed strange to have it and as Mother thought I should walk to the store and the lake, I didn't use it very much.

There were no children to play with right at the Center and sometimes I missed my Saco schoolmates. Len Doughty had told me about his niece and nephew who lived near the

Pond Lily Cove across the lake, so I began to wonder if I couldn't ride my bicycle up there to see them. It wasn't very far, just a little over two miles and Mother, Susan and I had walked there once or twice.

One day Mother took Susan with her to get eggs at Mrs. Warren's and I suddenly decided to start off on my bike without telling anyone. I knew this was wrong but I thought I would just ride up quickly, say "hello," and come right back. The road followed the lake for a little way and I could look through the trees to the water. It always seemed strange to see the familiar shore from this point of view. It was really more fun in the boat, I knew, because the road was dusty and in places it was so sandy that I had to pump hard to make any headway. There was one hill where it was easier to get off and wheel my bicycle.

Agnes and John Haskell's father ran a sawmill on a wide brook that flowed into the lake. As I rode toward the mill, I could hear the whir of the big round blade cutting through a log and, as I came out of the woods, I saw Agnes and John skipping flat stones at one end of the dammed-up pool where pine logs were floating. We called "hello" to each other and they came over to meet me. Agnes was about my age and had red hair and lots of freckles, but John was a little older and darker. They both smiled as if they were glad to see a new playmate. They looked with interest at my bicycle and I wiped some of the dust off with the hem of my dress so that they could see the pretty red-and-silver color.

"Would you like to ride it?" I asked.

They both nodded eagerly so I sat down by the pool to

cool off and they each took a ride around two sides of the pool. When John came back, he pulled out of his pocket a handful of small dark chunks of spruce gum he had cut off a spruce tree that morning. It took some minutes of hard chewing to make the gum elastic and at all like the store gum I was more used to, but the flavor of spruce was strong and I liked it. When my jaw got a little tired, I took the gum out of my mouth and stuck it in my pocket. It had changed in color from dark brown to a quite bright pink.

John was very surefooted and I guess he wanted to show me how good he was at keeping his balance. He walked out on one of the pine logs in the mill pond and when it rolled slightly, he jumped to another log and stood upright on it while it spun around. He dared Agnes and me to try it but I was glad when she said, "No, let's go bounce on the lumber." She ran toward the piles of lumber behind the house and I tagged after her, but I couldn't run nearly as fast as she could. The lumber was stacked in even, horizontal piles with a small upright piece between each layer so that rain could run off and air get in. Agnes said it was piled this way so the lumber would season. She ran to one of the big stacks and showed me how to stand on a board near the bottom layer, and then, by holding a board that was as high as my head, I could bounce up and down on the flexible wood. It was a new kind of fun for me and when John joined us, we shrieked with excitement, running from one stack to the next in the hope of finding more springy boards. It was like standing up on a seesaw but with one end securely anchored.

I forgot all about hurrying home and, after a while, when

we were hot and breathless and John suggested we go into Mr. Haskell's icehouse to cool off, I ran along after him holding hands with Agnes.

The icehouse was just a little distance away at the other end of the mill pond and as we stepped inside, the cold air struck me like a freezing hand. I felt as if the cold smoothed down my skirts and wrapped them tightly around my legs. We had to shut the door after us to keep the warm air out, and it was a moment before I could see. The high stacks of ice were at the far end and right in front of us was a floor of ice. Light came through cracks between the boards of the icehouse and, though the ice was covered pretty thickly with sawdust, there were places where I could see the dark green, almost black surfaces. We could slide smoothly on the ice floor, taking a few quick steps and slipping along until we bumped into the wall.

We had just begun having fun and John was planning to climb up on the high stacks of ice when his mother opened the door and told us to come out at once. She was very angry and said the ice might have fallen down on us and broken our toes. She boxed John's ears hard and he winced and ran toward the house, and I suddenly remembered I ought to go home. I ran quickly to my bicycle, a little afraid Mrs. Haskell would box my ears too. I didn't stop to call goodbye but I started pedaling as fast as I could toward home.

When I reached the house no one was in sight. I wheeled my bicycle into the barn and put it in the empty stall next to Nellie's. I hoped Grandfather would not see it until I had had time to wipe off the dust. I looked with sudden dismay at my dress which was streaked with dirt and there was saw-dust in my shoes and in my hair. I had a very hollow feeling. Mother would not box my ears, I knew, but that made it all the worse. Perhaps she would not trust me again and I might lose my bicycle for good. Yet, deep down inside me, there was a new feeling that I couldn't explain. On my two long rides I had broken through the loving, familiar circle of people and things that protected me and I was a little more independent than I had ever been before.

NINETEEN

The Medicine Show

I was in the blacksmith shop one afternoon, standing by the wide open door. It was a hot day and the breeze, which blew through from front to back, smelled of charred wood and of the hay in the field behind. A buckboard drawn by two thin gray horses that kicked up a cloud of dust stopped by the door and a red-faced man, wearing a derby hat and a short coat that was very tight, leaned over the wheel to call out, "Say, how do I get to Tompkins'?"

Sitting beside him was a thin woman who had on a long duster over a black silk dress. She was wearing black mitts and a black lace hat that was heaped with red roses. Her cheeks were bright pink and I guess she must have put some paint on her red lips.

In the back seat was a girl about eleven years old who looked different from anyone I had ever seen before. She had long smooth golden curls hanging halfway down to her waist and her short red dress was made of very thin silk. I suddenly felt that my straight braids and blue gingham dress were extremely plain and somber.

Mr. Tompkins was a farmer who lived across the road from the blacksmith shop and who occasionally took boarders. I stood by Mr. Sawyer as he directed the man over there. The girl smiled at me and tossed back her curls.

The back of the buckboard was crowded with boxes and trunks. "That's costumes and medicine," the man said in a loud hearty voice. "Here you are! These tickets will get you into the show," and he handed two tickets to Mr. Sawyer and passed two down to me. I wondered what the tickets were for and then I suddenly remembered a poster I had seen in the store which said that Leslie Peterson and his talented family would present a show in the schoolhouse and also sell Compton's Elixir, guaranteed to cure rheumatism.

The school building in Waterboro was the high school and also the town hall. It consisted of just one large room. There were two doors at either side of the front of the building, one for boys and one for girls, but they both led into the same narrow hallway where there were rows of hooks for coats and lunchpails. In the main room, in the summer, the desks were piled back in one corner and along the side walls so that the center of the hall was free for square dances and meetings.

Benches and campstools were placed in rows for the

Petersons' show which was to take place every night for a week. There were not enough people in our neighborhood to fill the hall, but I guess farmers and their wives drove in from miles around because a show almost never came to our village. Mother walked up with Susan and me and we were lucky enough to get seats near the front. There were quite a few other children there and some women brought their babies.

There was a platform at the back of the schoolroom and one corner of it had been screened off with a green curtain that was strung on a rope fastened to the wall and a window-frame. The Petersons got ready for the different parts of their show in this corner.

First, Mr. Peterson came out wearing a costume like Uncle Sam. He had black-and-white striped pants, a red vest and a long coat. On his head was a glossy tall hat. He announced that Mrs. Peterson, a famous concert singer, would begin the program. He then pushed out a little organ for her to play on and she appeared wearing a dress like Columbia the Gem of the Ocean. It had a skirt with wide blue-and-white stripes and her hat was red, white and blue. She played and sang "In the Gloaming" and "The Last Rose of Summer" and finally some lively Irish songs.

Then the girl came out in the red silk dress. The skirt was very full and very short. She had on thin-soled, black shiny shoes. She whirled and danced from one end of the platform to the other while her father beat a drum and her mother played a banjo. I thought it was the most amazing thing I had ever seen. When she finished everyone clapped and I clapped so hard my hands smarted. She made a deep bow and threw a kiss.

Much of the time of the Petersons' show was taken up in selling Compton's Elixir. Mr. Peterson tacked up a sheet over the school blackboard, set up a magic lantern halfway down the room and then showed pictures of people whose rheumatism had been cured by this wonderful medicine. There was an old man in one picture who was all bent over, but the next picture showed him standing up straight with a pitchfork in his hand. There were pictures of women, too, who seemed to have been made very well with Compton's Elixir.

Mr. Peterson then said that anyone who bought a quart bottle was entitled to five votes for the prettiest baby. In no time we were divided into those who wanted the Clough baby to win, and those who were for the Tibbetts baby. The winner was to receive a silver cup at the end of the week. Mr. Peterson held up the cup at each show.

The Clough baby lived near us so I begged Grandfather to buy some of the medicine for his rheumatism and then he could vote for the Clough baby. I felt very badly when he said he didn't think the medicine would do him any good.

When Mother saw how eager I was for the Clough baby to win, she suggested that I ask Mrs. Clough to let me wheel her baby past the store at mailtime and also past the blacksmith shop so that everyone could see her. Mrs. Clough thought this was a good idea and let me put on the baby's prettiest bonnet. But in spite of this, I knew by the third day that the Tibbetts baby would probably win because I saw her father buy two cases of elixir down at Tompkins' where the Petersons were boarding.

However, this contest did not interest me nearly as much as Gwendolyn did. I found out her name the first night and I soon made her acquaintance because she came to the store in the morning and then walked slowly by our house. Mother suggested that I ask her to go swimming with us at the lake and when she said she would like to but didn't have a bathing suit, I gladly offered her mine and Mother hunted up an old one for me.

We were the only family that used the lake for swimming. The neighbors thought it was strange that we liked to go into the cold water. Nearly every afternoon, after the mail stage had passed, Mother, Susan and I walked through a field down to a grove of pine trees and through them to Grandfather's boathouse which was built on a little cove that had a narrow sandy beach. Mother usually sat on the bank and watched us and sometimes, I guess, we frightened her by holding our noses and staying underneath the water as long as we could.

Gwendolyn was so slender that Mother had to pin the bathing suit together in the back with safety pins and I noticed for the first time how bony her elbows and knees were. The water seemed awfully cold to her and I was disappointed that she couldn't swim and duck under as I did. She said she had to keep her curls dry and that her hair was really straight so her mother put it up on rags every night. It took at least half an hour to do this.

It wasn't until we had gone swimming for several days that I noticed Gwendolyn's underclothes. Susan and I were used to undressing in opposite corners of the boathouse, hanging our clothes on hooks and slipping into our bathing suits quickly without looking at each other. Gwendolyn made us feel shy by standing around with all her clothes off. One day Gwendolyn's dress fell off the hook and I saw her underclothes which she had hung carefully underneath the dress. Her waist and petticoat were clean but yellow from being very old and worn. There were patches in the petticoat and holes in the toes of her stockings. She snatched up her dress and hung it quickly over the underclothes and then we raced each other to the water.

Gwendolyn talked a lot the first two days telling me of the many towns she had seen and how, when she grew up, she expected to be a famous dancer in Boston and New York. I listened enviously.

When Mother saw how well Gwendolyn and I were getting along, she asked her to have dinner with us and after that she spent every day with me except for an hour of dance practice in the morning. I lived in a strange world all the week.

Mother let me go to the show three times. She walked up with me twice and once I went with Mrs. Jones. This was most unusual as my bedtime was nine o'clock. Gwendolyn said she never went to bed until eleven. Going to a show of this kind even once was a new sensation for me. I had been to church entertainments that the Sunday school teachers arranged and tableaux at Christmas time, but they were not very exciting. The previous winter in Saco the tableaux had represented famous hymns. I remembered well one tableau that was about the Rock of Ages. A girl much older than I was supposed to cling to a wooden cross. The cross would not stay upright and I volunteered to lie, completely concealed, under a green rug and hold on to it so it wouldn't tip over. I got warmer and warmer as the choir sang verse after verse of the hymn. I didn't think Gwendolyn would think much of that. I had also seen "Uncle Tom's Cabin" when it came to the Biddeford City Hall and for days afterward I had shivered at the remembrance of little Eva escaping across the ice from the bloodhounds.

It was a strange idea to me that a girl so near my own age could have a life so different from mine, but I tried to show Gwendolyn my favorite good times. One day I rowed her to the pond lily cove. She didn't sit in the middle of her seat and I had to move from one side to the other to keep the boat balanced. I told her if we kept very still we might see a blue heron, but she talked too much. We picked a bunch of the sweet-smelling white lilies for her mother and one for my mother. Gwendolyn put a lily behind each ear and looked at her reflection in the still water.

Another day I took her up the hill to pick blueberries. She sat on a big flat rock facing the distant view of the White Mountains. She picked and ate the berries on the low bushes around her feet but she didn't try to fill her pail.

Gwendolyn was surprised when I told her we only stayed in Waterboro Center for the summer. I told her I had to go back to Saco each fall to go to school. She said she went to her grandmother's in Bangor for part of the winter and went to school there but she didn't like it. When she was there she spent several hours a day practicing dancing and her dancing teacher was very cross. But she explained that she had to work hard to become a famous dancer. As I sat beside her on the flat rock, she told me funny stories of people who had come to the show in different towns and she mimicked their way of talking. We laughed so hard we rolled over in the grass and I felt sure she and I were going to be good friends all our lives. It wasn't till we started to walk back that I noticed she had on tight, pointed shoes which must have been uncomfortable in the rough pasture. I wondered if she had had a good time but as we separated at my house she said, "Thank you for taking me."

One day when it was raining, and we couldn't go swimming, I took Gwendolyn up in the attic. The rain was pattering down softly on the roof and the swallows in the parlor chimney were twittering. I opened the big chest of old-fashioned clothes and Gwendolyn looked at them with great interest. She smoothed the heavy silks and picked up a pale gray silk dress that had belonged to Great-grandmother Peavy. I urged her to put it on. The skirt was very full and had rows and rows of ruffles. The waist was tight with little tiny velvet buttons down the front. Gwendolyn's waist was so small she could fasten it easily—something I could never do. Suddenly, holding the skirt high with one hand and waving a black lace fan with the other, she started to dance a minuet. I clapped my hands in time to her steps.

"Didn't you ever learn to dance?" she asked me.

I told her that I had been to dancing school in Saco but I didn't say that I had gone for only one winter. I thought of that dancing class with its polite rules and I felt sure Gwendolyn would be scornful of it. I had been proud of my pretty challis dancing-school dress. It had little sprigs of flowers on a cream background and rows of narrow black velvet braid on the sleeves and hem, but there was nothing about it as exciting as Gwendolyn's red dress. I carried my dancing shoes to the class in a navy blue flannel bag and never wore them any other time as Gwendolyn did.

"Can you kick up over your head?" Gwendolyn asked.

"I never tried," I said honestly. "At the start of dancing school," I explained, "we had to walk with our partners up to the chaperones and make a bow and then we stood in line to learn the steps of the polka and schottische." I could see that Gwendolyn didn't think that was much fun.

"Your little sister is pretty," she said. "I'll bet she could dance."

Quickly I remembered with pride that Susan had been in a Japanese play at the May Festival for the benefit of the Saco Hospital. She had to run onto the stage with little tiny steps and twirl a parasol. I tried to make this seem like a big affair.

When we came downstairs Gwendolyn stopped by my bedroom door. She didn't say anything for a minute but stood looking at my comfortable big bed. On the wide pumpkin yellow boards of the floor were the bright hooked rugs that Aunt Addie had made. Through the nearest window we could see the green field stretching down to the pine woods. Long streamers of rain were falling.

"Its nice here," Gwendolyn said with a little shiver.

"Do you have to drive on to the next town if it is raining?" I asked.

"Oh yes," Gwendolyn said proudly. "We always keep our engagements."

Later that day after Gwendolyn had gone, I got Susan to go with me to the hayloft and we practiced kicking. Susan did quite well but when I tried to kick over my head I always fell. I wondered if I could ever learn to be a dancer.

On the day following the last show, Gwendolyn and I had a short swim in the morning because the Petersons were leaving for Limerick right after dinner. Gwendolyn was eating dinner with us, as she had done all week, and Mother had made a big blueberry pie for dessert. I was busy eating the juice with a spoon when I noticed a tear slip down Gwendolyn's face. She quickly wiped it away but in a minute she was sobbing. Suddenly she jumped up and gave me a quick hug and, without saying a word, ran out of the room, across the porch and down to Tompkins'.

"Why, what's the matter?" I asked Mother in bewilderment.

"Would you like to leave your friends and go to a strange new place every week?" Mother said quietly.

I hadn't thought of it that way, but then I remembered how Gwendolyn had liked my room and how she had said that they didn't always know just where they were going to stay when they arrived in a new town. I looked around our sunny dining room and somehow I didn't want to be a famous dancer quite as much.

"Whoa there!" called a voice and looking out we saw the

Peterson buckboard stopping by the door. Mother went outside with me. Mr. and Mrs. Peterson were sitting in the front seat and Gwendolyn, with her face all streaked with tears, was in the back. "Thank you, ma'am, for being so kind to Gwendolyn," Mrs. Peterson said.

For the first time I noticed that Mrs. Peterson's dress was faded and that Mr. Peterson's coat was badly stained.

"Oh, I wish you didn't have to go!" I called earnestly.

"Come again next year," Mother said, and with that Gwendolyn smiled and nodded vigorously. The horses started and Gwendolyn and I waved as long as we could see each other. Then, suddenly, all my mixed feelings caught up with me and I was crying on Mother's shoulder.

TWENTY

The Brass Button

It was on rainy days when I couldn't play out of doors that I discovered the treasures in the attic. The main attic consisted of one big room, unplastered, with the ceiling sloping down steeply on both sides from the high center peak. Several thick beams went across from side to side and were fastened with wooden pegs instead of nails.

There were two windows at each end, but the room was so long that it was dark in the middle. Two big chimneys went up through the attic, their bricks were a faded, soft pink and the chimneys slanted so that snow could not easily fall all the way down. Beside each one was a low box filled with sand to catch any rain or snow that might leak in during a heavy storm. Over the ell of the house was a dark pocket where the ceiling was so low that I knew I would bump my head if I ventured in there. The kitchen chimney filled much of this corner and Grandfather said there might be a bat or two keeping warm and sleeping by this chimney. The boards of the attic floor were very wide and must have been cut from trees much bigger than any I had ever seen in Grandfather's woods. Mother pointed them out to me one day and said that much bigger trees used to grow around Waterboro Center and that my great-grandfather had had all the lumber for the house cut from his own woodlots.

When I first went into the attic, I was running away from Susan. We were playing hide-and-seek and I was looking for a new place to hide, but I only climbed halfway up the attic stairs and sat there with the door closed at the bottom. I was half scared to go up all the way. Then, later, as I got used to the soft light slanting in from the side windows, I went up the rest of the way and discovered the big chest filled with old-fashioned clothes!

Aunt Addie and Mother had pinned little pieces of paper on many of the dresses and I read that the heavy black silk dress with its velvet trimming and tight little waist had been Aunt Addie's wedding dress when she was eighteen years old, and a lovely pale gray silk dress had belonged to Aunt Lu. There were some long, fine, wool stockings embroidered with pink-and-blue flowers which had been Grandmother's wedding stockings and there were two little head coverings which Aunt Addie called "fascinators." They were crocheted of coarse white wool with a ruffled red edge and were just big enough to cover the front of a lady's hair. The crocheted strings tied under her chin.

There were hoop skirts in the chest and two silk dresses which had very wide skirts that were meant to be worn over the hoops. I tried on the largest dress which was made of brown, shiny silk and there was a quilted bonnet to match it. The waist was very tight and the hoop skirt kept swinging up in front of me and was hard to manage. I found a small, white paisley shawl with a lavender-and-black border and a very thin embroidered white mull fichu with which I could cover the place where the dress didn't meet in front. The little flowered poke bonnets were fun to put on and so were the black silk mitts. Once, when I was all dressed up in the brown silk dress with the bonnet and the mitts, I sat down in the sitting room with some sewing in my hands and I kept my head down as Grandfather came in. I may have looked as Grandmother used to for Grandfather stopped short and said, "Very good, very good—but don't wear these clothes out of doors." He must have guessed that I was planning to go over to show Mrs. Jones.

When I became curious for the first time about the contents of some of the other old trunks and about the old tools which were near the front window, I asked Mother to come up and tell me about them. There was a foot warmer to take to church when there was no heat, a candle mold for making candles, a wheel for winding yarns and under the eaves was a big box filled with small, hand-whittled pegs to be used in putting soles on shoes. On the beams were some iron hooks from which Grandmother had hung strings of apple quarters so that they would dry for winter cooking. And there were several sturdy firkins painted dark blue, or red, in which sugar or flour used to be kept.

Mother told me that everything painted that special red had been made by the Shakers. She thought the red dye came from the sumac blossoms. She told me to run downstairs and see how many Shaker things I could find and I discovered our sitting-room table was Shaker red and so was the one in the kitchen and so were the kitchen chairs. The dark red rockingchair with a split bottom that was in the dining room had come from the Shakers, too. I ran to the kitchen closet and looked at the oval wooden boxes in which Mother kept tea and coffee and spices. These, too, were Shaker red. I had been to the Shaker Village once with Mother, but I hadn't known that so much country furniture was made by them. Mrs. Jones had driven down to take two chairs to be recaned, and Mother had a chair that needed a new seat too, so we went along with her.

Shaker Village was only five miles away on the Alfred Road. There was a shop in one end of a big barn that was as clean as a house and there were two plain white buildings without any blinds. The women and girls slept in one of them and the men and boys were in the other. As we drove up we could see a number of men and boys with long, straggly hair weeding in a large vegetable garden. A woman in a gray dress and a gray cap came out to see us and she said they would do the chairs for fifty cents each. In the shop Mother bought a sewing box for Susan and one for me. They were made of thin wood that was polished but not painted and were lined with pink silk. There was a small, pink silk pincushion sewed to the lining of each one and in each was a very small, sweet grass container for a thimble. The flagroot candy which Mrs. Jones bought was both bitter and sweet. I didn't like it very much.

One rainy day in the attic I opened one of the heavy Shaker chests which I had not explored before. It had hinges made of small squares of leather and was filled with bulky ledgers dated 1837. The writing was small and neat and the "S's" looked like "F's." These were account books which Great-grandfather had used in his store. I also found a trundle bed under one of the windows. Neatly tied and piled up in it were copies of *Frank Leslie's Ladies' Magazine* for 1862 and 1863. The pictures of the fashionable ladies looked like the daguerreotypes of Great-grandmother in the parlor.

There was a heavy maple bed near one of the windows and on it were piled two feather beds and three or four quilts whose patterns of squares and triangles had been cut from bright calico materials used by Grandmother long ago. On stormy days I liked to lie on this bed, with the raindrops pattering on the roof very close to my head and the swallows twittering in the parlor chimney, and look at the pictures in *Godey's Ladies' Magazine* or imagine what it must have been like to live in this house all the year around as Grandfather and his brothers and sisters had done before the Civil War. I wondered why Grandfather had ever left Waterboro Center.

Aunt Addie told me he had moved to Saco when Mother was two years old and Uncle Byron was five. "Maybe," Aunt

Addie said, "he wanted his children to have a better education than they could get in the one-room school in Waterboro Center." It was true that our Uncle Byron, who was now a doctor in Colorado, had been to Harvard Medical School and then spent a year in Vienna and Mother had gone to boarding school and to Europe for a year but surely I thought nothing could be so wonderful as living in Waterboro Center. I thought this even more when I made my big discovery.

Way in under the eaves of the attic, I noticed one day a small trunk covered with leather of a mottled brown color. The initials "J.L." were on the cover made by nails with large round brass heads. I pulled it to the light and opened it. On top were some yellow newspapers. They were the Boston *Tribune* for 1863. Under them was a long brown cardboard box tied with a faded white ribbon. I opened the box carefully, wondering if I ought to look. Inside was a beautiful white satin vest with a pattern of twining leaves in the rich, heavy material and under the vest lay the blue coat of a soldier. The blue material was fresh and unworn and the gold braid was only slightly tarnished.

I was so excited that I almost tumbled downstairs in my search for Grandfather. "Why, yes," he told me. He knew about the vest and coat. They had belonged to his brother James. He had been a lieutenant in the Union Army. The vest was his wedding vest—only he never got married. He went to California soon after the war and died out there. Grandfather acted as if he didn't know any further details. His voice was husky as he told me to "run along." I ran back to look at the box again and I took the coat close to the light where I could see its beautiful blue color. I felt in the pockets but there was nothing in them. Then I noticed that a brass button was missing from the front of the coat. It was the third one from the top. I felt carefully in the box and trunk but could not find a loose button. Where could this button be? The coat was almost new. Certainly it had not ever been worn when Great-uncle James was in battle. How had the button come off?

One day Mother and Susan and I went for a long walk to pick blackberries. There were lots of blueberries in the fields near the house and beside the roads but blackberries were different. The ones that grew on low vines along the ground and tripped us up were not very sweet, but those in the high bushes in the woods were juicy and delicious and were hard to find. Grandfather had a secret spot which he would not show to anyone, but Mother guessed it was on one of the low ridges of the mountain where an abandoned road was overgrown with alders. When she asked Grandfather if he thought there might be berries there, he said, "Well, maybe," and his eyes twinkled as he passed me his favorite pail.

It was a long walk but we did find the bushes full of berries and they were so big and firm that our pails were soon full. We had brought some sandwiches with us and we sat down on some moss to eat them. Our backs were against a big hemlock and the air was sweet with the smell of our berries.

Before starting back for home we decided to explore a half-hidden path that seemed to lead across a brook and through some birch trees. Two rotting logs had once been put across the brook to make a bridge but we felt safer stepping on the flat rocks that stuck up out of the water. We pushed the low branches of the trees aside and to our surprise we came to a clearing in which four or five old apple trees were growing. The apples on them were very small and green and the tree trunks were gray and covered with lichen. A little further along was an empty cellar with the stones of the foundation tumbled into a heap inside and tall pink fireweed growing over the rocks. We decided a barn must have stood here once. Beyond this was an abandoned house; its clapboards, which once had been white, were now black, its windows were broken and the front door was missing. Orange day lilies were in blossom along the foundation, and a knotted old lilac bush bent halfway over the door.

The house looked as if it was settling into the earth. A branch of the maple tree beside it was lying along the roof. Grown into the maple tree was a rusty spike where someone, long ago, had tapped the tree for sap, and a few links of a chain hanging from a branch had once been part of a child's swing.

We walked nearer and looked in the windows. The rooms were bare, but squirrels had made nests in the corners and a porcupine had lived there recently. I wanted to go inside and, after promising Mother to walk very carefully on the sagging floor, I stepped over the threshold. I hesitated by the stairs that went up steeply from the narrow hall, and then cautiously mounted.

Upstairs were three bedrooms and, after testing the floor, I went into the nearest one. The room had once had wall-paper with a pattern of blue morning-glories. Small patches

of the paper remained on the walls and the boards of the
floor, which were very wide, had been painted a matching
blue. The ceiling was low and sloping. There was one window that looked toward the mountain, and the sun was
streaming in. There was nothing in the room, but I tiptoed
across the uneven floor and opened the closet door. It was
dark and smelled musty. Then a bright ray of sunshine fell
on the floor, and I saw something gleam in a crack. I knelt
down and looked more closely. There was a button stuck between the boards. With a loose nail I pried it out and took
it to the window. I recognized at once that it was the same
size and pattern as the buttons on Great-uncle James's coat.
The minute I got outside, Mother knew something had happened. I held out my hand, too excited to speak.

"I wonder," she said, and then paused and said nothing
more.

The walk back seemed very long, and when we came in
sight of the house and saw Grandfather hoeing in his garden,
I couldn't walk slowly any longer. I put my full pail in
Mother's hand and ran the rest of the way.

"Grandfather! Who used to live in the old house on the
side of Durgin's Ridge, the house behind the place where we
pick blackberries?" I asked.

"It was the old Hobbs place," Grandfather said.

"Did Uncle James have a friend there?"

Grandfather was silent for a moment, and then he said,
"Lovey Anne Hobbs lived there. She was the girl James was
going to marry."

I tried to get more information from him but he answered

each question with a brief "yes" or "no." Mother tried at suppertime, but all Grandfather would say was the Hobbs family had moved away years ago, after their son was killed at Gettysburg.

The next morning Mother suggested I ask Mr. Sawyer about the Hobbses. I ran all the way to his shop. Yes, he remembered Lovey Anne. She was a pretty girl whom all the young men liked. He remembered James, too, and the fast sleigh that he drove and how he would race other drivers over the frozen lake. He had often seen Lovey Anne sitting beside James with a big buffalo robe over her lap and she would be laughing and holding up her muff as they skimmed along.

"What became of her?" I asked. But Mr. Sawyer didn't know.

The button seemed like a great treasure to me and I carried it around with me for the rest of the summer. Sometimes I kept it in my pocket and sometimes it was tied in my handkerchief. I knew it could have come from some other coat, but I called it Uncle James's button.

I often went up in the attic and untied the box to look at the beautiful blue coat. I pulled the button out of my pocket and placed it beside the other buttons on the coat, and I wondered when and how Great-uncle James had given it to Lovey Anne. Once I lost the button for a whole day in the haymow in the barn. I was almost in tears but Susan helped me push the hay around until we saw the edge of my white handkerchief and pulled it out. Once I left it tied in my handkerchief on a branch of the big pine by our boathouse and Mother walked down with me in the early evening to get it.

The last day of vacation finally came and I had to decide whether to take the button to Saco with me. It had gone with me around the lake and up the mountain. It had been in my pocket as we drove away from the house when the forest fire was coming. I had often shown it to Mr. Sawyer at the blacksmith shop in the hope that I would learn more about Uncle James and Lovey Anne. I had shown it, with pride, to Gwendolyn when the medicine show came to Waterboro Center.

Now it was time to go down to the boathouse and say goodbye to the lake and to the mountain. I went up to the attic and took out the coat once more and smoothed it gently on my lap. When I looked up, Mother was standing by the stairs. She held out a spool of blue silk and a needle. "I thought you might like to sew the button back on the coat."

I took the needle and thread without saying a word. Mother did not wait to watch me. As I threaded the needle, she went down the stairs.

I didn't sew very well, and my hand trembled. The thread knotted and broke several times, but at last the button was in place. I folded the coat carefully in its box and shut the little trunk. I tiptoed across the attic floor and down the stairs. At the foot of the stairs I gently closed the door. The summer was over.